Heart
Connections

By Gordon MacDonald
   Ordering Your Private World
   Renewing Your Spiritual Passion
   Rebuilding Your Broken World
   Christ Followers in the Real World
   Rediscovering Yourself
   There's No Place Like Home

By Gail MacDonald
   High Call, High Privilege
   Keep Climbing
   Parenting: Questions Women Ask

Gordon and Gail MacDonald are the parents of two grown children. Gordon, a popular lecturer and conference speaker, was formerly president of Inter-Varsity Christian Fellowship and now serves as pastor of Grace Chapel, Lexington, Massachusetts.

Heart Connections

Growing Intimacy in Your Marriage and Family

Gordon and Gail MacDonald

Fleming H. Revell
A Division of Baker Book House Co
Grand Rapids, Michigan 49516

© 1992 by Gordon and Gail MacDonald

Published by Fleming H. Revell
a division of Baker Book House Company
P.O. Box 6287, Grand Rapids, MI 49516-6287

Paperback edition published 1997

Previously published under the title *Till the Heart Be Touched: Building Intimacy in Marriage, Family and Friendship*

Printed in the United States of America

Library of Congress Cataloging-in-Publication Data

MacDonald, Gordon.
    [Till the heart be touched]
    Heart connections : growing intimacy in your marriage and family / Gordon and Gail MacDonald.
       p. cm.
    Originally published: Till the heart be touched. Grand Rapids, Mich. : Revell, c1992.
    ISBN 0-8007-5635-5 (pbk.)
    1. Man-woman relationships. 2. Intimacy (Psychology) I. MacDonald, Gail.
II. Title.
[HQ801.M345 1997]
158.2—dc21
                                      97-25998

This book is based on the principles first presented in *If Those Who Reach Could Touch* by Gail and Gordon MacDonald.

To a loving and courageous woman,
Ethel Scott Akerlow,
Gail's mother

And in remembrance of a man
who was a credit to his generation,
George Walter Akerlow,
Gail's father,
who now enjoys being in the presence of Jesus

We will always be grateful for their
support through the years.

And in appreciation to the Revell Family

Contents

Introduction

Thou only hast taught me that I have a heart—thou only hast thrown a deep light downward, and upward, into my soul. Thou only hast revealed me to myself; for without thy aid, my best knowledge of myself would have been merely to know my own shadow—to watch it flickering on the wall, and mistake its fantasies for my own real actions. Indeed, we are but shadows—we are not endowed with real life, and all that seems most real about us is but the thinnest substance of a dream— *till the heart be touched.*

Evan S. Connell, Jr.
Mr. Bridge

We met as college seniors. A mutual friend introduced us with the curious comment, "I think the two of you could build a great marriage." Words like those would bring almost anyone to a state of alertness. They did for us, and so we shook hands and came out talking.

Within a few days of that first encounter, we found ourselves agreeing with the assessment of our friend and began to merge schedules whenever possible. In three weeks we were engaged to be married; in five months there was a wedding. That was more than thirty-two years ago. This chronology is neither common nor recommended, but that's what happened with us.

9

If you want to know how our relationship sprang to life so quickly, the explanation is simple: Hearts touched soon after hands were shaken, and something called intimacy ignited. It wasn't a mature or deep intimacy at first. But on the other hand, the two of us, Gail and Gordon, made a convincing connection, and we set out to forge an enlarging communion that would last till death and, along the way, gain the capability to survive even the most crushing blows.

Intimacy is, unfortunately, an often misunderstood word. To many it has only sexual connotations. But to clamp that narrow a limitation on the word is to cheat it of its fullness. Intimacy is something much, much more than sex. It describes what happens when people's hearts touch and their spirits are fused in a unique and powerful friendship.

Intimacy focuses upon a great human need to be heard and understood, as well as to hear and understand. It is not a cheap word, because genuine intimacy is something attained only at great cost. It takes a lot of intense work to learn to know another person and to allow oneself to be known in return.

When does intimacy happen? Since a complete definition is hard to pin down (but you know it when you have it), it's hard to be precise.

In our experience, we felt we were discovering intimacy when it became clear that we shared a common goal in life. We both wanted to give our generation more than we might take. We knew intimacy was in process when something within us cried out, "This is the person you want to be with, share your life with, give your life to. This is a person you'll enjoy, in whose success you will delight. This is a person whose God is your God, whose vision is your vision, whose mind engages with yours."

We found intimacy when we took the risk of divulging some of our inner feelings and noted, to our relief, that the other person treated the disclosure with unusual respect and sensitivity. Intimacy resulted when we talked and found it instinctive to be positive, truthful, inspirational, and life-giving with each other. That wasn't true all the time, of course, but it was much more than in conversations we'd had with others.

Finally, we knew intimacy was in the air when we felt the wish to see the other person grow in the fullness of everything God wanted them to be as a person. We saw intimacy blossoming when we felt the other's hurts, when we wanted to pray together, search the Scriptures together, and serve God and His people together.

All of this was intimacy, and we've been building it through the years since we commenced our marriage, raised our family, and now are taking our first enthusiastic steps into grandparenting. The process of intimacy building never ceases, and the flow of rewards is splendid.

Yet despite our joint commitment to building intimacy, there have been some very tough times. While we have shared many peak experiences, we've also known intense anguish, for there is risk in the building of intimacy, and there can be failure and hurt. We've known that failure and hurt!

Intimacy achieved yesterday is no guarantee of intimacy tomorrow. Although intimacy is dynamic, quite capable of expanding, it is just as capable of contracting and being lost or forfeited. It's clear to us now that what one builds, one guards. Intimacy is a delicate treasure between two people in a marriage or a friendship. It cannot be assumed or taken for granted.

If there is a danger in the pursuit of intimacy, it may lie in our attempts to find in another human being what we were meant to find in our relationship to the Creator. The fact is that our full craving for intimacy will only be realized in God Himself. If this is not understood, then a person may seek—sometimes even demand—what it is impossible for another to give.

There are many kinds of relationships between people, and not all of them include intimacy. The novel (recently a film) *Mr. Bridge*, from which the romantic prose of the first paragraph of this introduction is drawn, is the story of a Kansas City lawyer and his family: husband, wife, and three children. The Bridges display all the marks of stability and success—on the surface. They enjoy an orderly home, a busy social schedule, regular vacations, classy schools, and faithful attendance at church. But within this seemingly prosperous family, there is no convincing connection between people, except for the superficial words and interplay that modern life requires. If there had been intimacy in the earliest days of the Bridge marriage, it was lost in the rush to succeed, impress, and accumulate. Thus Mr. and Mrs. Bridge went their own ways, and hearts stopped touching. "All that seems most real about us is but the thinnest substance of a dream—*till the heart be touched.*"

So went the conclusion of Mr. Bridge's romantic message to his bride—a message he wished to convey to her, but didn't. The words never left the paper upon which they were written, and Mrs. Bridge never found out how badly her husband wanted to know her and how badly he wished to be known. He simply could not bring himself to say what he felt in that early flush of love, and Mrs. Bridge never found a way to decode the signals of his heart.

The result? Their three children grew up unable to have nourishing relationships with anyone, since as children they'd not witnessed one. Mr. Bridge was locked in a loneliness he could not admit or define, and Mrs. Bridge found herself trapped one winter afternoon, slowly freezing in an automobile as she feebly cried out to no one in particular, "Is there anyone there? Is there anyone out there?" There was no answer.

Sadly, we can have marriages without intimacy, families without intimacy, friendships (or rather acquaintances) without intimacy—no commonality of goals, no openness, no communication, no desire to build and serve—only the visible framework of relationships in obligation, responsibility, and appearance.

We are writing from personal experience. We know what it is to build intimacy, to lose some of it, to rebuilt it and renew it with daily regularity. We know what it is to succeed and what it is to fail.

This is a joint effort. We have loved doing it, because the ideas spring from the core of our lives, the thing we originally set out to do: build a relationship that keeps intimacy alive.

We're grateful to those who have encouraged us to re-address this matter. It would have been easy to drop the subject, thinking we really had nothing to more to say, but it has been shown to us that when a couple builds a relationship, discovers their bonding can survive any shock and actually gain strength as a result, perhaps there *is* more to be said.

Everyone starts life with high hopes of loving and being loved, knowing and being known, building and being built. This is true not just in a marriage, but also in friendships where there is genuine community, a touching of minds and hearts. But then, for many people, somewhere along the way something goes sour, and more than a few become bewildered, dispirited, defeated, and maybe even bitter. Does that mean that one just quits?

No. If there is still a desire for intimacy, hearts can indeed touch and be touched, and that's what builds intimacy.

Gordon and Gail MacDonald

INTIMACY
HAPPENS
When
the
Heart
Is
Touched

1
What This Is All About

Gordon: *I'm thinking of one of the darkest days of our lives.*

Gail: *You mean the day you told me that you'd been carrying a secret?*

Gordon: *Yeah. I'd lived with that secret far too long, and I'd become terrified of revealing myself to you.*

Gail: *Even though we had promised each other that honesty would be one of the center points of our marriage?*

Gordon: *Yes, I know we had made that promise, but at the time it seemed easier to keep a secret and hope it would never be found out.*

Gail: *I could tell something was terribly wrong.*

Gordon: *How could you have known?*

Gail: *You may not have realized it, but a part of you removed itself from me, and I began to hurt badly. There was a wall of some kind building between us. It was a wall that had never been there before, and I knew it had to come down.*

Gordon: *That's why you finally pushed me to disclose the secret?*

Gail: *I knew that everything we had worked for in our relationship was in jeopardy. Not necessarily because an awful wrong may have been done, but because it was not being surfaced and accounted for between us. Anything can be endured if two people face the truth together. What destroys intimacy in a relationship faster than anything is allowing an issue to go unnamed and unacknowledged.*

Gordon: *You made it possible for me to open my heart to you, even though it was a moment of maximum pain for both of us.*

Gail: *I think God had been preparing me for that moment. You and I had spent years building a relationship capable of taking a heavy blow. Maybe if we hadn't done that building from the very beginning, it would have been a different story.*

Gordon: *I would rather lose my life than go through that day again. But the mercy and kindness I discovered in your love changed me forever. God took a terrible thing and squeezed redemptive results from it.*

Gail: *There have been other times, Gordon, when you've paid a high price for me. That's what intimacy is all about.*

If food is fuel for the stomach, intimacy is fuel for the soul. Without the one, there is physical starvation; without the other, there can be spiritual starvation.

Intimacy implies a deep and lasting connection between persons. You might think of it as a kind of energy flowing between two or more people. Intimacy is expressed in a score of ways between good friends, teammates, marriage partners, and family members. There is even intimacy between a person and God. Age, intellect, class, gender, and all other such classifications are all irrelevant when it comes to experiencing this intense rapport.

Yet some of the most intelligent and powerful people in our lives appear to know almost nothing about intimacy. They may be able to baffle us with brilliance and charisma; they may be able to write or speak and make us believe that they care and that they want to be our closest friends. But get this kind of person alone, one-on-one, and you may discover that his or her capacity to connect on an intimate level is virtually nonexistent.

In contrast to this, the simple, the young, and even the emotionally handicapped give and receive intimacy in ways that amaze us.

One of our favorite books is the biography of D. E. Hoste, a great missionary leader in China (*D. E. Hoste* by Phyllis Thompson, CIM Press, 1947). When he was heavily burdened, he would walk back and forth in the garden behind his office, his lips moving in silent prayer as he sought answers to seemingly unsolvable problems.

The writer of the biography tells how a child saw him walking one day and became curious. Her mother firmly told her daughter not to bother the great man, but that didn't seem to faze her. The biographer puts it this way:

> She was unaccountably drawn to this man of whom older people were often rather afraid, and when he saw her and held out his hand, she ran forward instinctively to slip her own into it. The warm confiding touch of her little hand in his gave a sense of release to his spirit, and as he continued to walk up and down, prayer flowed on in a steady stream, while the child trotted quietly and contentedly beside him. She was about five, and he was nearly fifty, but what did that matter? They trusted each other, and as he poured out his heart (in prayer) for matters far beyond her understanding and interest, she heard her own name mentioned.
>
> "Mr. Hoste prayed for me this morning!" she announced when she returned to her mother. And when she was rebuked for bothering him, she said in simple justification, "But he held out his hand!"

The older man and small child found a slice of intimacy. You can't observe this kind of connection in a test tube, and you can't analyze it statistically on a computer, but you know when it happens. Something within you, far beyond words and reason—something in the environs of your soul—indicates when intimacy is happening. To borrow a phrase, you feel God's pleasure.

Why do so many men complain of a lack of friendship? Why do so many married couples speak of a closeness once possessed but now lost? Why do many young people complain that their fathers or mothers never knew them? Why is it that pollsters, therapists, and poets all seem to agree that loneliness—the opposite of intimacy—is the most frequently mentioned problem when people take a hard look at what's missing in their lives?

At the age of twenty-four, Arnold Beisser, a superb athlete and medical student, contracted polio, which confined him to an iron lung for an extended period of time. He writes of his sense of total isolation (*Flying Without Wings*, Bantam, 1990):

> I rarely had physical contact with non-hospital people, they did not touch me, they did not shake my hand, they did not reach out in any physical way. They were probably afraid that they might hurt me or catch what I had or perhaps they feared that they might do something wrong and appear foolish. I was unable to reach out myself so there remained a physical gulf between me and others in the world. It was lonely, and I longed to be touched.

In his autobiography, playwright Moss Hart tells of the same kind of feeling. He recalls a childhood Christmas when his father took him shopping. The two walked the New York streets, inspecting the merchandise displayed on scores of pushcarts. Hart's eyes were drawn to chemistry sets and toy printing presses. His father, a poor man, had less-expensive things in mind, but was reluctant to say so.

Each time they would find something the boy wanted, the father would ask the vendor's price, shake his head, and move on. Occasionally he would pick up a smaller, less-expensive toy and try to attract his son's attention, but there was no meeting of the minds. Eventually they came to the end of pushcarts without making a purchase.

Hart writes:

> I heard [my father] jingle some coins in his pocket. In a flash I knew it all. He'd gotten together about seventy-five cents to buy me a Christmas present, and he hadn't dared say so in case there was nothing to be had for so small a sum. As I looked up at him I saw a look of despair and disappointment in his eyes that brought me closer to him than I had ever been in my life.
>
> I wanted to throw my arms around him and say, "It doesn't matter. . . . I understand. . . . This is better than a printing press. . . . I love you." But instead we stood shivering beside one another for a moment—then turned away from the last two pushcarts and started silently back home. . . . I didn't even take his hand on the way home, nor did he take mine. We were not on that basis. Nor did I ever tell him how close to him I felt that night—that for a little while the concrete wall between father and son had crumbled away and I knew that we were two lonely people struggling to reach each other. (Quoted in *A Creative Brooding* by Robert Raines, Macmillan, 1977.)

Why do some find it so difficult to connect? Why, in this case, does a father find it awkward to acknowledge both his hopes and limitations? Why does a son quench his desire to say what he feels? Why can't this boy and his dad hook up, especially when that is exactly what they both desire and need?

21

We Were Made for Intimacy

We're reminded of our need for intimacy every time our attention is drawn to a television commercial that features lovers looking fondly at each other, friends embracing each other at an airline terminal, estranged family members reestablishing contact over the telephone, or a small child walking hand in hand with a grandparent. We are drawn to that strangely intimate moment when athletes lose their inhibitions in the flush of success and shower one another with unabashed affection. The theme of intimacy is reverberating within when we are brought to stillness by the words and music of a love song or the picture on the front of a romantic greeting card.

The profit-driven communications industry knows how hungry we are for intimacy. Advertising in the 1990s, we are told, will lean heavily on our increasing sense of loneliness. Strange! We possess all these marvelous gadgets that facilitate communication: FAX machines, computers with modems, E-mail, overnight package and mail delivery, fiber-optic telephones with call forwarding and call waiting, answering machines, quick and relatively cheap transportation, and laser printers with graphics capabilities to enhance and illustrate our messages to each other. Yet we're lonelier than ever.

You could say that we have the hardware for intimacy but lack the software: the program that permits the heart to be reached.

Intimacy became an issue the moment we were born. Perhaps intimacy was never better than in the womb, where the developing child rests secure, warm, nourished, tucked up under the mother's heart. That's why it is important that a newborn child be placed instantly on its mother's stomach, its mouth at her breast. The baby reaches out for the security, nourishment, and warmth it has known within the womb.

There is strength in this intimate connection, and it is far more than just the life-giving substance of the mother's milk. In these earliest moments of life, the baby experiences its first feelings of acceptance and belonging, simply by the way he or she is cuddled.

Edmund Janss, a physician who has spent most of his life among the poor in the developing nations, writes:

> On St. Thomas Mount in Madras, India, I once watched a housemother tenderly holding a baby. She was feeding her while humming a gentle song. The baby had been found on a trashheap crying weakly. I asked the house parent about her feeding method. She nodded and said, "If we don't hold them and sing to them while we feed them, they often die." (*How to Give Your Children Everything They Really Need*, Tyndale, 1979.)

Those babies are not unique. As we learn more and more about ourselves, we discover that being touched is basic to health and perhaps even to survival. William Glasser, an often-published psychiatrist, suggests that "psychiatry must be concerned with two basic psychological needs: 1) the need to love and be loved and, 2) the need to feel that we are worthwhile to ourselves and others."

As the child grows a few months older, it discovers that intimacy means other things, also. It learns to respond to affection and friendship. How these needs are fulfilled will have a great deal to do with the emotional health of a child during the teen years.

Alan Loy McGinniss writes of a friend who has a four-year-old daughter who wanted to hear the story of the Three Bears every night at bedtime. His friend, being technology oriented, had a great timesaving idea. He simply read the story into a tape recorder and presented her with the cassette. But she was not at all pleased.

"Now, honey," he said, "you know how to turn on the recorder."

"Yes," she said, "but I can't sit on the recorder's lap." (*The Friendship Factor*, Augsburg, 1979.)

In a book entitled *Touching* (Harper and Row, 1971), Ashley Montagu includes the words of Kabongo, a Kikiyu chief from East Africa:

My early years are connected in my mind with my mother. At first she was always there: I can remember the comforting feel of her body as she carried me on her back and the smell of her skin in the hot sun. Everything came from her. When I was hungry or thirsty she would swing me round to where I could reach her full breasts; now when I shut my eyes I feel again with gratitude the sense of well-being that I had when I buried my head in their softness and drank the sweet milk that they gave. At night when there was no sun to warm me, her arms, her body, took its place; and as I grew older and more interested in other things, from my safe place on her back I could watch without fear as I wanted and when sleep overcame me I had only to close my eyes.

James J. Lynch, a leading specialist in psychosomatic medicine at the University of Maryland, argues that social isolation (lack of intimacy) brings emotional and *physical* deterioration. Disease, he suggests, can be loneliness induced. Lynch stresses the importance of the family and of caring relationships with friends and neighbors. "Simply put, there is a biological basis for our need to form human relationships. If we fail to fulfill that need, our health is in peril." (*The Broken Heart: The Medical Consequences of Loneliness*, Basic, 1979.)

Intimacy remains at the center of the journey as a child crosses into adolescence. There are exultant moments and despairing moments as great experiments in intimacy are conducted. There are the youthful romances, the shifting of best friendships, the stormy interludes with parents.

In this process, you hope that the teenager's quest for closeness will become balanced and appropriate and that eventually there will be more giving than taking. For that is one of the great objectives of the noble life: maturity in which one seeks to serve others. The process of maturation in intimacy may be the most important single matter of personal growth and development.

One of the great issues that aids or deters the growth of intimacy is that of secrets and what we do with them.

Through painful experience, the two of us discovered what we knew in theory. If you permit a secret to enter the relationship and remain unconfessed, unacknowledged, and unresolved, a corrosive effect invades the relationship. What had been a constant convergence toward greater intimacy becomes a gradual divergence away from it. One partner has a fear of being "found out." The one who doesn't know the secret begins to hurt, but doesn't really know why. What is known is that something has slid into the space between them— something like a wall. Suddenly the energy of intimacy isn't flowing quite as powerfully as it once did.

This need to be known is the way God has "wired" us. Unfortunately it doesn't take too many years for us to begin to put on our masks and play a part with each other.

Although it is instinctive to want to receive the fruits of intimacy, the capacity to give intimacy probably has to be learned. For two hearts to touch, we must give *and* receive, talk *and* listen, share *and* see into another. No one can or will do all of that unless they have been taught and are motivated. That's what this book is all about.

Gordon: *You know, Gail, I really believe all we've said in these first pages. I believe it with all my heart. What amazes me is that a person can think they believe this kind of thing and yet still fall into the trap of secret carrying.*

Gail: *Scary, isn't it? Perhaps it's easier for some to fall into that trap than for others.*

Gordon: *Yeah, and I'd say it's easier for me than for you. As an introvert, I've lived in a quiet world of my own and have probably not always been as candid as I should have been. I've had to learn to be more open about what I'm thinking and feeling.*

Gail: *I'm working hard at giving you every opportunity to do that.*

Gordon: *I guess that's why that wall that was there for a short while years ago was shattered. It's not there now, and I'm grateful.*

Gail: *Me too!*

2
How Do You Make Hearts Connect?

Gordon: *One of the greatest gifts you have given me, Gail, is the knowledge of how to be a friend.*

Gail: *What makes you say that?*

Gordon: *Well, I look back on the days before I met you and realize that I knew a lot of people, but I didn't know how to be friends with them. Franky, I used people, and I guess I dropped them the moment they seemed irrelevant to my life.*

Gail: *That sort of makes it hard to be close to anyone, doesn't it? And when you needed a friend?*

Gordon: *When I needed a friend, there weren't many around, except maybe one or two who liked me in spite of my selfishness. I'm not sure I ever stayed in one place long enough in my youth to understand the importance of committing to a relationship, nourishing it, and being willing to give, even if it meant giving more than I got back.*

Gail: *I grew up in just the opposite sort of world. The people around me were extremely generous with their time, their possessions, and their compassion.*

Gordon: *I remember being astonished at the number of cards you received on your birthday and the cards we received that first Christmas.*

Gail: *Those were from friends. I've tried to maintain those relationships—some closer than others—down through the years.*

Gordon: *I know. I see the postage and phone bills every month.*

Gail: *But that's one of the prices—one of the less-expensive prices—one gladly pays for caring and support.*

Gordon: *A lot of folks convince themselves that they're too busy for that sort of thing.*

Gail: *They may wake up later in life feeling terribly lonely and remorseful that they don't know anyone well.*

Gordon: *Well, that's why I'm grateful. I think I've avoided that sadness, thanks to you. But you're right! It takes time; it takes energy; it means setting some priorities.*

Gail: *And look at the friends you have now!*

In an autobiographical account of his business life, T. Boone Pickens talks about the struggles he and his wife, Lynn, had in their marriage.

> [We] had different interests. That was easy to overlook when I was a high school basketball star and she was the prettiest girl in the class. But after ten years looks became less important than compatibility. I cared passionately about my work and wanted her to take a greater interest in it. I had a sense of humor and admit that I was sarcastic at times. But instead of laughing at my jokes, Lynn disapproved of them.

According to Pickens, the relationship began to deteriorate.

> Most troubling of all, she often just said nothing. I remember nights at home after the kids were in bed when I would try to start a conversation about something that had happened during the day. She would say, "That's interesting." She was unhappy—maybe she didn't know how unhappy. I probably should have forced the issue. (*Boone*, Houghton Mifflin, 1987.)

The touching of two hearts—intimacy—usually happens slowly, over time. While we long for it to happen and happen quickly, most people do not know how to make it happen or have the patience to let it happen over a period of time.

One person struggles with intimacy because he or she never saw examples of it in the family when growing up. Another is terribly hurt in a relationship where intimacy had begun to grow but was destroyed by a betrayal or tragedy. As a result, many men and women say, "Never again will I get into a position where my heart can be hurt so deeply."

Harold Kushner recalls a teenage girl who, sitting by the bedside of a boyfriend dying of cancer, is asked by the nurse, "Is there anything I can do for you?" She answers, "Yeah. Remind me never to love anybody this much again."

We have heard psychologist Larry Crabb say, "We long for relationship and because we long we hurt." Unfortunately, the "hurts" can snuff out the longing—at least a healthy longing for connectedness.

The Disciples and Intimacy

The two of us are committed to biblical living, so when we wanted to know something about intimacy, we went to the Scriptures.

We started with Jesus. No one comes close to His capacity to give and receive intimacy. His was a world known for its cruelty, abuse, and human exploitation, the opposite of intimacy in every way. But Jesus cut through all of that. He knew how to connect with soldiers, businessmen known for flagrant corruption, women of high and low reputation, children, servants, and religious leaders. He never pushed Himself on anyone. In fact He seemed prepared to sever relationships with anyone who was not interested in dealing with total integrity.

Among the things for which Jesus will always be noted was His successful attempt at taking twelve disparate men and building a team out of them. It took three years before their relationship began to generate effectiveness, but when it did, that base of rapport they had built together became the cradle of a movement that altered history.

What was the secret of this team intimacy? Jesus said, "A new command I give you: Love one another. As I have loved you, so you must love one another. By this all men will know that you are my disciples, if you love one another" (John 13:34, 35 NIV).

This statement is the centerpoint for intimacy in all human relationships. Jesus obviously wanted to teach His disciples about a totally new kind of relationship.

We can hardly appreciate the drastic difference between how Jesus related to His disciples and what those men had known previously. They lived in a world of brute power, blatant racism, and minimal charity. Jesus' wish for them— that they become a team of bonded men—is clearly revolutionary. It calls for an intensity of connection men had rarely known before.

Males had known strong connection in battle and were familiar with the loyalties of tribal and family lines, but this was something new—a caring, nourishing, building love among men, women, and a mix of men and women. This was a love that might cause one to lay his life down for another. It was, in fact, revolutionary.

The disciples were by no means perfect. There had been ideological rivalries; there had been competition for status in the small but burgeoning movement; there had been concern about who would be remembered as the greatest among them; there had been moments of volatile anger and outrage, such as the day a few of them wanted to bring fire down upon a village that refused them hospitality.

The twelve had frequently demonstrated insensitivity toward suffering and poverty, and soon after Jesus spoke these words they would illustrate that their courage was quite limited and, given a chance, they would disappear rather quickly.

Although the disciples were well-meaning men, they tended to be relationally incompetent. Nearly two thousand years later, people have not dramatically changed for the better.

But the disciples did change. That disjointed group of competitors and squabblers became a good team. In their development in this area, they remind us of what you see in the end zone when a football team has scored. Eleven men pile on one another, exchange "high fives," hug, head slap—generally make fools of themselves in the midst of their joy. They've done something together; they explode with excitement, with appreciation for one another, with a celebration of bonding. "We've done a great thing, and we kind of love one another," you can almost hear them say.

How did Jesus teach intimacy to His men? Pick apart His words to the disciples about loving one another, and you discover three salient issues.

The disciples had to be *commanded* to love one another. "Choose to do it! Love them!"

The first principle Jesus taught for developing intimacy through love was, choose to do it. The second was, act it out. This love He willed for them, which would grow into intimacy, was modeled (acted out) first by Jesus Himself, by His proactive love for them. As Jesus established a loving, intimate connection with them, they were to establish the same kind of connection with one another. This was no small thing!

Finally, if these men could generate such friendship among themselves, a witness of startling proportions would be generated. A world that craved such closeness would be amazed by what it saw in the disciples and their followers, and would be drawn to Jesus as a result. In their life together, the message would be plain for all to see: Intimacy—the kind for which the human soul cries—is possible. And that's what happened; the world saw that very thing. In detail, what did it see?

It saw a new generosity. People placed at one another's disposal any necessary resource in a time of trouble—money, food, shelter, even the laying down of life. It saw new kinds of friendships. The older and the younger drew strength from one another; the strong and the weak supported and leaned on one another. It saw a new kind of organization. People worked together for the common objective of seeing the world reached with this good news. It saw new families and marriages. Men and women treated each other with dignity, respect, and servanthood; children were stamped with special value and esteem. It saw new ways of relating in business. Masters treated servants as brothers; employees gave their employers a new level of productivity; those entering into contracts kept their word. The evidence of faithfulness and intimacy in Christian relationships was simply unimpeachable.

Scott Peck begins one of his books, *The Different Drum* (Simon & Schuster, 1987), with an old story. A monastery was in trouble. The monks were old, dispirited, and fearful that the life of their order was almost over. In the midst of a furious search for some solutions, the abbot went to visit a rabbi. The rabbi quickly assured the abbot that he had no advice to offer, but he did feel compelled to say, as the disappointed abbot was about to leave, "The Messiah is among you." Neither knew the significance of those words, but the rabbi pressed them upon the abbot once again: "The Messiah is among you."

The abbot returned to the monastery with only that cryptic comment to offer the curious monks. At first no one responded to the rabbi's words, but then questions sprang to life in the minds of the monks. *Suppose the Messiah really is among us. Who might he be? This monk to my right? That monk to my left? Could I possibly be the Messiah?* A new air of mutual affection and respect swept among the monks. Their care and treatment of one another, their desire to know one another better, took on a new seriousness. Who knew when he might be talking to the Messiah?

The monastery changed. It became a bright and wonderful place for outsiders to visit. Soon young men asked to join the order. They wanted to be part of a place where there were genuine bonds among people. What they were drawn to was a form of intimacy, the kind of powerful connection that Jesus was talking about to His disciples.

Intimacy Lost

Where did this quest for intimacy begin? If we are "wired" to give and receive it, why is it so hard to master? The Bible, in its earliest pages, provides an answer.

The Book of Genesis describes a magnificent garden where the first man and woman made their home. Their ability to communicate and experience companionship seems to have been unlimited. How long they lived like this we don't know.

But what is clear is that the first man and woman made an unfortunate series of choices. They chose to violate God's simplest laws, and the result was devastating. Intimacy—the close connection of people and systems of creation—was dealt a crippling blow. It was as if everything that had been created to be in harmony suddenly fell into conflict and dissonance.

The first loss of intimacy resulted in estrangement from God, with whom the first man and woman had enjoyed unbroken communion. It is written that God came searching for them and found them hiding, ashamed of their choices, strangely embarrassed over their now-naked appearance. For the first time, they had something unfortunate to hide, a secret they wanted to keep from their Maker, and that seriously diminished their relationship with Him.

When God entered the garden that day, Adam and Eve were nowhere to be found. It is almost amusing to visualize Adam in the bushes, hoping God could not find him. What had previously been a beautiful fellowship was now something to be avoided. Adam and Eve were humiliated. They'd tried what they thought was a superior way, and now they didn't want to account for the results, so they hid, thinking they could keep their choices a secret. Ever since that day, humankind has tended to hide from God, but still He comes in search of us. God is forever seizing the initiative to reestablish intimacy with those who choose to stop hiding.

It is also obvious that a second intimate relationship was shattered—that of Adam to himself and Eve to herself. You could say that a part of each person declared war on another part. Each was filled with excuses and faulty explanations. Each was no longer a fully integrated person, each part of self no longer intimate with the other parts. The man once created as whole was no longer whole.

We see the same tragic decentralization in our own inconsistent behaviors. A person may intellectually agree with the data that says smoking causes cancer. But another part of the same person will crave the narcotic effect of tobacco and choose to smoke. You may tell yourself intellectually that you ought to attach your safety belts in your car, but you may ignore that fact because using them may be inconvenient or uncomfortable.

Because of disobedience, the third possibility for intimacy—that between Adam and Eve—was also shattered. They began to blame each other when the heat was turned on. Adam refused to accept responsibility for his own actions. When he put the blame upon Eve, Adam suggested that she was something less of a person than he; that he could have gotten along without her. What a far cry from the grateful man who, seeing Eve for the first time, had cried out, "At last; this is bone of my bone, flesh of my flesh." But now, in a sudden moment of defensiveness and resistance to repentance, Adam displayed for all humanity the proud heart that blames others for the consequences of deeds and attitudes, even if it effectively destroys connection between people. Adam and Eve's once intensely intimate relationship simply ceased to exist.

Today we inherit that same attitude. Each time we transfer blame for our actions to others, we are simply repeating the choice Adam made when he backed off from Eve in an attempt to clear himself.

Adam and Eve also forfeit the privilege of a fourth kind of intimacy because of their disobedience—their connection with all of creation. The Scriptures teach that before evil entered the world, humankind enjoyed dominion over the living things of nature. To work in such an environment meant discovering and appreciating what God had brought into being as a reflection of His own glory. Now, God told them, you will have to wrestle with nature for whatever you get out of it. It will no longer be subservient to your command.

Evidence that humankind has lost a sense of intimacy with nature is abundant in our lack of respect for creation. As a people, we have exploited the earth, draining it of its natural assets, spoiling its beauty, and littering it with our waste. In the vivid imagery of pollution we see not only what we've done to creation, but what we have done to one another.

There is a biblical suggestion of a fifth shattered form of intimacy: the ways in which nature ravages itself. All of nature seems to have somehow been touched by the poisonous quality of evil's power. As a result, nature would no longer fully reflect the glory of the Creator, as it had been designed to do. From that time forth, everything man would touch would be strangely stained, losing its reflective quality. So serious a matter was this that Paul would later suggest that all of creation awaits, even cries out, for the redemption of the children of God, for only then will creation be restored to its original condition: that of reflecting the glory and majesty of God.

When Adam and Eve disobeyed God, creation became a loveless place. The quality of relationships once enjoyed in the garden would not be seen again in such brilliance until Jesus Christ came bringing a new burst of the love that had once characterized time and space. This was the kind of love that He wanted the disciples to be careful to implement in their relationships with one another. The oneness originally experienced in the garden was the oneness Jesus desired for the disciples.

Today we struggle in our pursuit of intimacy because of those shattered relationships. That old, old story from the garden explains why we feel such a strong urge for intimacy and why it so often eludes us. We were made to enjoy intimacy with God our Maker, with ourselves, with one another, and with our world, but much of what we were made for simply isn't working as it was intended.

Lacking intimacy, we become like a battery-driven toy or tool that is running low on power. We have great capacity to function, but because our power is strictly limited, so is our performance.

When Jesus Christ instructed the disciples about a new intimacy, He was calling them to an effectual repudiation of broken relationships and to embrace a new quality of oneness with one another. He knew that the contagion of the new order would be tremendous, and so it was.

When intimacy was devastated in the garden, God forced the issue. He set in motion a revised system of relationships, one where—if His power were reinstated in the heart of any willing person—intimacy could be possible again.

Gordon: *Have you noticed that no matter how often we commit ourselves to the development of intimacy with friends, family, and each other, it's not long before we begin to violate our commitment again?*

Gail: *I'd have thought that by this time in our lives, we'd have learned the lesson once and for all.*

Gordon: *I think it has something to do with the overall system in which we live. Everyone in the marketplace, in the church, and wherever else, puts a premium on busyness, activity, and achievement. We find ourselves applauding and admiring the people who travel a lot, work the hardest, accumulate the most.*

Gail: *And yet if you permit yourself to get into that sort of life-style, you know the first thing that goes.*

Gordon: *Right: The connection of hearts.*

WITHOUT
COMMITMENT
The

Heart

Cannot

Be

Touched

3

Everything Starts With Commitment

Gordon: *You know who I think about every time we entertain a group of young men and women?*

Gail: *You're going to tell me about Verne and Marilyn again, aren't you?*

Gordon: *I never get tired of remembering what they did for me, because it pretty much changed my life. I was a college freshman. Verne and Marilyn were a newly married couple who came to the campus representing a Christian organization.*

Gail: *And they opened their apartment to you.*

Gordon: *Well, not exactly. I think I opened up their apartment to me. Somehow I managed to drop by their apartment at noontime almost every day.*

Gail: *Which was about the time they were sitting down to lunch.*

Gordon: *Exactly. And they would always invite me to join them. I'll never forget those lunches, because they used that time to pump their lives into me. They taught me some of the most important lessons I ever learned about hospitality, being generous, and even how men and women get along with each other. Those were wonderful times at the lunch table.*

Gail: *Did it ever occur to you that you were intruding on their*

> *privacy as newlyweds or that feeding you on their limited income was quite a sacrifice?*
>
> **Gordon:** *Only after I left school. I don't think I ever adequately thanked them at the time. I don't think it ever hit me that I must have been a real nuisance—if not a real bore. But they never let on that I was an intrusion.*
>
> **Gail:** *Isn't that because they were committed to you?*
>
> **Gordon:** *They were committed, all right. Even when I let them down—and I often did—they kept taking me back. If I had a quarter for every cheese sandwich they served me, I'd be a rich man.*
>
> **Gail:** *You are a rich man. Anytime someone commits to you as much as Verne and Marilyn did, you're as rich as anyone could ever be.*

In a recent highly publicized case, the defense lawyer attempted to persuade the jury that what the accuser called rape was actually a sexual event involving mutual consent. "Here are two people who met in a bar late in the evening," he said, "spent a couple of hours together, came back to the man's house, and decided to make love."

Whatever actually happened that night, the phrase "to make love" hardly describes the meaning of the contested event. Two people may have been involved in a sexual event, but "love" was not made.

All of us understand that the English phrase "to make love" has become a euphemism for sexual activity. As they say, the lawyer was trying to put the best possible "spin" on a tawdry moment, but he did it at the expense of the real meaning of the words *making love*. Making love cannot happen until one specific thing has happened first: commitment.

People may engage in sexual activity and call it lovemaking or even intimacy, but calling it that does not make it that.

Breathe!

Want to hear about commitment? Some years ago Nelson Pendergrass and his wife extended an invitation to a sixteen-year-old boy who had been in repeated trouble with the authorities. They invited him to their home, convinced they could make a difference in his life through the sheer power of love. "I thought I was the kind of man that could help him change," Pendergrass later wrote.

But nothing worked! David did not respond to the people-building climate of the Pendergrass home; in fact, he seemed to grow more resistant to relationship. Things became so bad that Nelson Pendergrass felt he had failed and David would soon have to be returned to juvenile court. He dreaded the decision, but each day the possibility came closer.

Then life suddenly changed and the decision was postponed, when a serious accident sent Nelson to the intensive-care unit of the local hospital. While recovering from his injuries, a blood clot approached his heart. Instantly, Pendergrass was fighting for his life.

Nelson wrote, "I gasped for air. But it hurt too much to breathe. Better to just drift away, I told myself. Away from the fear, from the pain, forever."

An attending nurse detected his thinking, and made the difference.

". . . there was [this] nurse, her face not six inches from mine. 'Breathe. You've got to breathe,' she said.

" 'Leave me alone,' I wanted to scream. 'Let me die.' But no, she was still there, and now she was shouting: 'Breathe . . . breathe . . . breathe . . . breathe.' I was willing to give up, but she was not. Again and again, I fought to take a breath as she called to me."

Nelson Pendergrass made it through the crisis that day, but the thanks, he says, belonged to that nurse who insisted that he keep breathing when he wanted to quit.

Not many days afterward, Nelson began to connect the crisis in the intensive-care unit with his disheartening experience with David. Should David be returned to the jurisdiction of the juvenile court? After all, he was showing no evidence of concern for what happened, so why, Nelson found himself reasoning, should anyone else care?

But now he had a new thought. When it came to David's situation, wasn't he in the same position as the ICU nurse who had coaxed and prodded him back to life? Wasn't he now in a position to confront this boy and shout an equivalent of the nurse's "Breathe!" That blunt, self-directed question caused the foster father to decide that he would present David with another chance.

But before he could do so, there was another crisis. David was arrested for stealing a car, and Nelson was called to the police station. When the two met in the holding cell, there was clearly no response on David's part. His first reaction was to tell Nelson to leave him alone, to get out of his life. But this was unacceptable to Nelson Pendergrass.

"David," he said to the boy, "as long as you're under my supervision, you're not giving up on life. And I'm not giving up on you, either. We're not quitting. You're coming home. And you and I and the Lord are going to get through all of this."

David went back to Nelson's home. The crisis dissipated, and as the next months passed, the Oklahoma rancher and his foster son rebuilt their relationship. Something must have worked, because today David is a husband and father, a responsible and productive human being. What you see in

David today began the day a man made a commitment to a younger man to convince him to "breathe." (Story told in "Our Blue-eyed Maverick," *Guideposts*, November 1982.)

Genuine intimacy begins with such commitment: a stepping across a line into an alliance. One chooses to engage another and to pay whatever price is necessary to achieve the purpose of the relationship. That's what Nelson Pendergrass chose to do with David; it's what Jesus chose to do with His disciples. It is *not* what the couple opposing each other in the courtroom rape case chose to do.

Among the people of our generation whom we most highly admire is Robertson McQuilken of Columbia, South Carolina, a man who knows about commitment. Not too long ago he withdrew as president of a college because of his wife's difficulties with Alzheimer's disease. He simply decided that the situation called for him to provide full-time attention to his wife, Muriel. "After all," he told a reporter, "she cared for me for nearly four decades; now it's my turn.

"Was it a right decision?" he responded to an interviewer. "Oh yes. It was a matter of integrity; I made the vows. And it's a matter of fairness; she served me. But she really is a most delightful person—very lovable. And although there's a lot of work involved in her care, she's always so grateful and cheerful.

"If sticking with my marriage depended on having my needs met, we wouldn't be married. None of these criteria apply in our situation. Communication? Very little. Understanding? None. Affirmation? Muriel can only speak the phrases 'I love you' and 'Thank you.' And common interests? We had many in the past but those are gone, along with the memories we shared. If we hadn't had such a wonderful marriage that wouldn't be such a loss. But she is a delight to me still."

Amazing, isn't it? Most people today would opt out of such stressful situations. We tend to look for loopholes that permit us to dissolve such a commitment. But McQuilkin has raised the standard back up to where it should be. He makes it plain that a commitment is a solemn thing, easily made when times are easy, a challenge to fulfill when times are hard. (Story told in article by Maggie Wallen, *The New England Christian*, EANE, April 1991.)

In her book *Traits of a Healthy Family* (Harper & Row, 1983), Dolores Curran writes:

> Dr. Bruno Bettelheim has given much of himself to families throughout the years, but perhaps one of his greatest gifts to us has been his assurance that good families have rough times. "A family doesn't prove itself through having a good time together," he reflects. "Your worst enemy will be willing to have a good time with you. You need your family when things are rough. Then children know what a parent is here for—to bind up the wounds, particularly the psychic ones. Realize that you can prove your worth to your mate or to your child only when things have gone wrong by sticking together and making things right. That's the best thing we can give our children, the hope and conviction that even when things get tough, we'll be able to cope."

Jesus had this kind of durable, strength-giving intimacy in mind when He invited twelve different men into a new kind of relationship. Encountering them one by one—mostly at their places of work and labor—He offered a unique friendship. "Follow me," He said, "and I will make you fishers of men" (Matthew 4:19 NIV). He was making a commitment to them even as He asked them to make one to Him. As each agreed to follow, he crossed a line. Three years later, Jesus would say of these associations, "I no longer call you my servants . . . instead I call you friends, for everything that I have learned from my Father I have made known to you."

If Nelson Pendergrass's foster son did everything he could to dampen the ardor of his surrogate father's commitment, the disciples were not far behind. They failed, misconstrued, and generally thwarted the purposes of Christ so often that He would have been quite justified in abandoning them. But He didn't, because He had made a commitment.

Every time one of those men failed Jesus, He seemed to say something like this: "I'm looking past this moment of failure to the day when you'll try again, and that time you'll get it right. I believe in you. Let's go! Now breathe!"

People today are frightened of this kind of commitment. They are frightened to make a commitment to a friendship that might ask too much time. They are frightened to make a commitment to a marriage that might inhibit their personal freedom. They are frightened to make a commitment to raising children, because their career might be jeopardized. They are frightened to make a commitment to God, because it might infringe on their perceived pursuit of happiness.

Jesus called the disciples first to an association with Himself and then to a similar association with others. He was challenging them to a connection that went beyond the normal cultural expectations of family, clan, or tribe. Men who had strongly differentiated temperaments, political sensitivities, and class status were asked to work together and serve one another in order to achieve a common goal. It could only happen if they made a commitment and then strived to fulfill what they'd promised.

Paul placed enormous emphasis upon the issue of commitment as a prelude to intimacy when he wrote to the new Christians at the Ephesian church. How do you teach a higher brand of commitment to people who have never seen it before in ordinary human relationships? His answer to that problem was to take a look at Jesus:

> Husbands, love your wives, just as Christ loved the church and gave himself up for her to make her holy, cleansing her by the washing with water through the word, and to present her to himself as a radiant church, without stain or wrinkle or any other blemish, but holy and blameless (Ephesians 5:25–27 NIV).

Paul equated commitment with a willingness to die for another person. That's what Jesus was willing to do when He gave Himself up for the church. These are not relationships at discount rates—ultimate costs are being talked about here.

Paul also uses the word *cleansing*. That suggests that commitment ignites a process of growth and development.

While this Bible passage is a magnificent description of the intimacy of marriage, it also applies to general friendships or family life. All relationships are only as healthy as the commitment that launched them. Earlier in this same writing, Paul said to all members of the Ephesian church, "Be servants of one another." This is not unlike what he asks of the Ephesian husbands.

In the gospels we read how Jesus committed himself to His disciples. What do we find? First, we see that He surrendered some of His own personal rights. Commitment always begins with that. The greatest of those rights was his own life as the Son of God in the center of heaven. He left heaven and came to earth in the form of a man. Someone has written:

> *Because we children of Adam want to become great,*
> *He became small.*
> *Because we will not stoop,*

He humbled himself.
Because we want to rule,
He came to serve.

A Modern Story of Commitment

Want to test the possibilities of commitment to its "nth" degree? Imagine discovering in the space of one hour that you have been infected with AIDS and your spouse is involved in a homosexual relationship. How do you handle the news and its implications?

Just a few years ago, David and Lisa Johnson were an average couple living in the Midwest with sons of two and four. One day Lisa entered the hospital with flulike symptoms that were weakening her entire physical system and would not go away. In fact, while she was in treatment, Lisa almost died.

After a modest recovery, but nevertheless while she was extremely weak, Lisa Johnson's physicians permitted her to go home. But she could not have known that the worst was yet to come. The night before her release, David gave Lisa a letter he had written to her. In its pages she discovered what David had been hiding throughout her recent illness: He had just learned he was infected with the AIDS virus, which he had no doubt unknowingly given to her. He went on to confess being involved in an extramarital homosexual relationship.

Lisa later told friends that David had fully expected her to react with hysteria. He'd even prepared for a psychiatrist to treat her. Furthermore, he was sure she would demand his immediate exit from their home, so he had already packed his bags.

But none of that happened. Although her heart was shattered, Lisa Johnson instantly chose forgiveness. She faced David with a question: "Do you love me?"

"Yes," he replied.

"Then let's work through this," was her conclusion. The couple began to put their broken lives back together.

Later Lisa would write of those first moments of horror:

> What could be a more confused situation? You are married and you are happy. You are secure. Suddenly, you become critically ill and you are at the lowest and physically weakest point of your entire life. Instead of the comfort and healing of the one you love most—you receive the most painful blow of your life. He loves you—but he also loves someone else. He would never hurt you—but he's killed you—he's ready to move out—but he doesn't "think" he wants to leave. He doesn't know anything anymore. And you feel like dying— now! This is a confused situation.

Making a complete break with his homosexual lover was no easy task for David, but eventually it happened, and their marriage began to find a new strength built upon mercy and forgiveness. The complications of the AIDS virus were always with them, but they refused to let this hideous disease or the cause of its transmittal become a destructive issue in their relationship.

When Lisa became ill again, it was clear the HIV virus was playing havoc with her body. They decided to share their secret with friends and members of the church they were attending. Some met the news with shock and horror, but others, astonished at the story of David's betrayal and Lisa's forgiveness, came closer. They wanted to understand and support this incredible effort at reconciliation and healing.

As the news of David and Lisa Johnson's extraordinary story

began to spread, many marriages were keenly affected. Here and there, some would say, "We thought we had problems in our lives. If Lisa and David can experience healing in their marriage, we can, too." Their lives became an inspiration to many who had forgotten that commitment means going the extra mile until all possibilities are exhausted, mercy has been extended to the repentant, and life's worst has been forced to produce good.

Lisa Johnson's body—but not her spirit—was finally defeated by the complications brought about by AIDS. As she lay dying, her closest friends gathered about her bed and sang hymns to her. Some said they literally escorted her into eternity. One of the nurses who attended Lisa in her dying hours told her friends, "You need to know of the impact that Lisa's death has had on our entire unit. We see so much death, and we have never seen people deal with it in this way."

The weaker Lisa became physically, the stronger she became spiritually. She wrote:

> The Good News of God to men is the only thing that gives me happiness. Grace reaching down to lift me up to truth—it's amazing. I have been broken . . . I have laid wounded. What causes my soul to rally is the hope that comes from knowing God and from believing that one day I will laugh all of this off as "present light affliction."

Before Lisa died, she insisted that her friends be reminded once more of how much she loved David and that she would never want anyone to blame him for her death. Forgiveness was complete.

At this writing, David Johnson is a seriously ill man. Their two sons now live with close friends who agreed to raise them after David and Lisa were gone.

No one who has heard the story of David and Lisa Johnson will ever forget it. It is a witness to what commitment means in the extreme sense. Not everyone would be able to do what Lisa did, but what happened will always be a benchmark as to what is possible when someone takes commitment seriously—a lot more seriously than many people in our age take it.[1] So this is where commitment begins—in the laying aside of our rights. It is what Jesus did, what Lisa Johnson did, what Nelson Pendergrass did.

This is where hearts begin to touch, where intimacy is ignited, where love actually begins to be made. When two or more people—in friendship, marriage, or family—cross a line and make a pledge to one another, you have commitment.

Gail: *It seems to me that commitment to a relationship means that it becomes my highest priority. It's a higher priority than winning, a higher priority than career, and a higher priority than being right in a dispute.*

Gordon: *And when there are drifts in the commitment, it's important to spot those drifts quickly.*

Gail: *You need to ask, "How did we get here, and what can we do to get back on track?"*

Gordon: *I think it's a good idea to make these appraisals of commitment on a regular basis.*

Gail: *Exactly. Then you can stop any slippage before it goes too far.*

---

[1] We are indebted to Michael Kelly Blanchard, whose song "Be Ye Glad" inspired Lisa to write of her joy in the midst of pain, and to Ann and John Shelton, whose friendship to the Johnsons has no human measure, for they are not only assuming responsibility for the Johnsons' sons but also are loving them as their own.

WITHOUT
TRANSPARENCY
The
Heart
Cannot
Be
Touched

4

Intimate People Are Transparent

Gail: *Do you remember the nonstop drive we once made from Florida to St. Louis? It was twenty-one years ago, but it still is as clear as a bell to me.*

Gordon: *I forget why, but the children slept most of the way, and that gave us a chance to do lots of talking.*

Gail: *I had been reading to you about Catherine Booth's painful death and how her husband, William, cared for her. I was overwhelmed by his tenderness during her long illness.*

Gordon: *Suddenly you began to weep and had to stop reading.*

Gail: *That scene brought up all kinds of memories that I had suppressed during the nine years we had been married. I suppose it was because I had been dumped by boyfriends in my teen years, but I wasn't confident that I could ever evoke that kind of love from you.*

Gordon: *I remember you saying that, and I remember how surprised I was that those fears were there. You hadn't talked about it before.*

Gail: *Perhaps I couldn't talk about it because deep down I feared you might dump me, too—especially if I became that ill.*

Gordon: *I was grateful that it surfaced so we could deal with it together.*

Gail: *Isn't it amazing that it took nine years of marriage for me to unearth it and find the courage to tell you?*

Gordon: *It surprised me then, but it doesn't now. All of us have all sorts of things swimming around inside that we're afraid to name, much less reveal to others—even, sometimes, to the one we feel closest to.*

Gail: *You handled me well that day. First of all, you created a climate of acceptance, asking questions, encouraging me to talk it through. You didn't ridicule me or make me feel childish.*

Gordon: *I recall thinking that you had trusted me with an admission of weakness, and it made me want to love you a thousand times more than I'd ever loved you before. It made me feel freer to unlock some closets of my own and give you a peek inside myself.*

Gail: *I guess if you only stay married for a few years—like many do these days—you never do find out what's deep within each other. Maybe it takes a lifetime to learn what's really in the soul of another person.*

Gordon: *The tough part, though, is staying open and accepting each other.*

Legend tells of an architect who offered to design a house for Plato. Assuming the philosopher had a taste for privacy, the architect assured Plato that no one outside would be able to look in. This he could do, he promised, for a remarkably low price.

"I will pay you twice as much," Plato responded, "if you design a house for me which permits everyone to see within."

That's transparency! It's the courage to let oneself be known (or knowable, as we like to say it): faults, flaws, virtues, dreams, pain, or delight—maybe more—with nothing consciously concealed.

Plato saw this new home as he saw his life, believing that if one has nothing to hide and lots of life to share, it might be better to enlarge the windows than downsize them. This principle of transparency is all too often overlooked or underestimated in the pursuit of intimacy in personal relationships.

Knowability

Transparency focuses on the question of how much we will permit others to know about ourselves. We could call it our "knowability factor." That would be the opposite of "unknowability," and to the extent that any of us is "unknowable" (and more than a few of us are), the quality of our relationships suffers.

Celebrities often seek notoriety, desiring to enhance what public-relations people call "the recognition factor." But these same people often end up hiding behind sunglasses and the darkened windows of stretch limos. Why? Because while they pursue popularity for career purposes, they are not interested in relational closeness or what we are calling intimacy. At least not with the people on the street. It's career advancement or money or political power they seek, not intimacy. These people probably would have welcomed Plato's architect's offer to build a house with one-way windows.

Nowhere is this false offer of intimacy more brazenly illustrated than in the world of pornographic literature and videos. There, on the pages and the screen, men and women act out the closest kinds of intimacy, offering to disclose their most personal sexual secrets. They seem to be saying, "Enter my circle of intimacy and privacy." But the promise always falls short. Those attracted to these overtures are usually titillated for only a short time. Then comes disappointment and hope that the next experience will offer something better. The way is paved for an incessant searching for the experience of intimacy without the risk of commitment.

Some, of course, are trapped by this pursuit of counterfeit

intimacy and succumb to sexual addiction. Once addicted, it is difficult for many to break the force of the drive, which dominates the heart and mind.

Most of us are not as sophisticated about knowability and recognition as public figures and their agents. But we are nevertheless concerned about how many people know us and how well they know us. Some people pursue intensely private life-styles, hoping for various reasons that few, if any, will discover much about them. Others appear to be in constant pursuit of attention, doing anything necessary to gain it. We will find ourselves somewhere in the middle of these two dangerous extremes.

Not long ago, in a series of TV commercials, semi-newsworthy people would ask, "Do you know me?" They would go on to explain that they often went unrecognized, and that, as a result, they carried a credit card as proof of identity. The message was clear: If no one knows you, a credit card is a handy thing to have in your pocket. It only costs 18 percent per month to be knowable.

We should indeed be concerned about how knowable we are. It is normal and right to want to be known and appreciated by a certain number of people within our circle of family and friends. We generally appreciate having those around us who will affirm us when we've done well, warn or chide us if they see us headed toward error, and share our sorrow or good fortune. We want to know that those who have looked deep inside us appreciate what they've found.

Problems of Knowability

Of course we will want the right to determine how far within us each of these people will be able to look. Everyone has had the painful experience of being transparent with a person and then having private information used against them. It doesn't take too many bad experiences to make us overly cautious.

An elderly acquaintance of ours misplaced a large sum of cash. We could tell that he was extremely upset, but couldn't appreciate why at first. Then we saw what was happening. His wife held the key to the situation. How would she treat him? She could either make this "their" problem to solve together or make him feel like an incompetent failure. She chose the latter. We watched her belittle him until he felt like a child who had misbehaved. You could tell that his windows were shutting rather quickly. She made it impossible to want to be transparent under such circumstances.

You can witness the opposite in meetings of recovering alcoholics. Recovery groups have done an incredible job of teaching us how to be "glass houses" or knowable. One night a group of us was each answering the question, When did you feel closest to God? Most of us were rather benign in our responses until a man who was a recovering alcoholic honestly shared how God had met him. The group melted in admiration of his courage. The next three men, also in recovery, who responded were equally transparent, each of them having learned the power of being honest with others and not playing games.

By the time that hour was over, all of us knew something very unique had happened because of these men's strength. They weren't afraid to be who they were, and they granted all of us permission to do the same. But their transparency was obtained at great cost: In each case, failure was the start of the redemptive process. As we prayed for one another that night, there was no pretense or shallowness in our intercession. But that would never have come about if it had not been for the first man, who was willing to risk our reaction to his story.

Sometimes one person in a relationship will volunteer transparency for the other, who is unwilling or unable to express himself. You'll find one putting words in the other's mouth, sharing secrets the other never meant to be disclosed, or telling the crowd how the other person really feels. Trouble! Not only is this a gross error in judgment, but it will also create further isolation on the part of the quiet one. We cannot be transparent for someone else.

Relationships suffer serious damage, however, when one of the parties chooses to avoid transparency at any level. More than once someone in a marriage has come to talk with us and related that the other spouse has rejected reasonable openness, blocking off large parts of his or her life. It can be a variety of things. "I don't know what he does with his money." "I don't know where he spends large chunks of his time." "I don't know what he thinks about me, about his job, or anything. We just don't know each other as well as I once thought we did."

To be sure, there may be many reasons for this sort of withdrawal. It may be the character of the one who has retreated into unknowability, but it may also be that the one who complains has previously mistreated the privacy of shared information, which can be equally damaging to a relationship.

All of us know people who successfully shade the windows of their lives. They do it by being extraordinarily silent, or, when conversant, making sure the conversation is always centered on anything but themselves, refusing to express feelings, hopes, dreams, or struggles. Sometimes they keep others at arm's length through the use of sarcasm, constant humor, or even expressions of anger.

It is not a simple thing to open our lives to others, yet until we do, we will never be ready for a relationship of high value.

Unwilling to be knowable, we will probably never enjoy a close friendship; it is possible that we will be frightened of making a marital commitment; and most likely we will never experience the joy of a team effort, where a group accomplishes something together. This matter of transparency is important. It should not be avoided, even though it is painful for some.

At the highest level of relationship—that of a person with his or her God—we will never enjoy spiritual intimacy until we have resolved this matter of transparency. No one who resists transparency will ever be able to say, "I know God."

Transparency Lost

The very first indication that there was something wrong in the relationship between the first man and God came when there was suddenly an absence of transparency on Adam's part. The Bible says that God came into the garden seeking Adam, but Adam sought to be "unfindable." He hid. There's no indication that Adam really understood what was bothering him, but he seems to have known instinctively that whatever it was, he didn't want the penetrating eyes of God to look at him.

He did the same thing with his wife, Eve. Trying to take God's attention off himself, he attempted to put the blame on Eve. In fact he tried to place the blame squarely upon the shoulders of Eve *and* God since, as Adam put it, God had placed Eve in the garden in the first place. Both in his marriage to Eve and his relationship with God, Adam became progressively unknowable.

Adam also ceased being totally transparent with himself. By

blaming Eve for his problems, Adam was lying not only to God but to himself, and when a person becomes wrapped in self-deceit, this is nothing more or less than a loss of transparency in one's inward life.

Friendships are not immune to this problem of unknowability. While there are friendships of varying levels and intensities and the depth of transparency will differ with every level, there still must be open windows into one's life. When there is not, friendship suffers.

Only in those relationships where there is an understood leader—such as parent to child or mentor to disciple—will the amount of transparency differ between the two people. A mentor will not necessarily share every detail of his or her life with a protégé, nor will a parent fully open all of his or her life to small children. That is neither practical nor wise. In this type of relationship, there will be selective transparency, with the wiser or older determining what is profitable for the other to know. There will still be some transparency, but in a more regulated or deliberate form.

There can be destructiveness in relationships where people resist proper transparency. In a "Peanuts" cartoon, for example, Lucy once told Linus that she felt unusually crabby, but she didn't tell enough of the truth so that Linus could appreciate the full situation. Based on what he did know, Linus innocently suggested he might be of help. Bringing her a sandwich, cookies, and milk, he wanted to know if there was anything he had not thought of, anything that could help her to feel better.

Now Lucy was forced to more transparency. "Yes," she said, "there's one thing you've not understood. *I don't want to feel better!*"

Linus had a perfect right to feel frustration and anger. He had acted on the basis that there was reasonable transparency, but there wasn't. He had taken time to reach out to Lucy, but he was unable to touch her, because Lucy wasn't adequately knowable. As a result, both she and Linus suffered.

Perfect Transparency

Jesus was a model of the transparent person. He was knowable to all who were interested, regardless of their economic status, gender, or spiritual orientation. When someone asked where He lived, He said, "Come and see." When someone came to visit in the middle of the night, He was available. When friends sought to entertain Him in their home, He went and enjoyed Himself.

Jesus made His feelings known to those about Him when He knew they could handle them. At the grave of friend Lazarus, He wept; with unjust prejudiced men at the temple, He expressed anger. On another day He rejoiced, and on still another He revealed enormous sadness over the rigidity of some of His critics.

The Lord was willing to speak of His personal objectives when questioned. He was responsive to those who came to Him seeking insight and wholeness. One of the most poignant pictures of His transparency was seen when a woman came to anoint His head with an expensive perfume. While others were critical and scolded her for what they perceived to be a gaudy display of adulation, Jesus protected her. She alone had looked into His life, He said, and had seen the suffering that was about to overwhelm Him. He thus permitted and affirmed her display of affection, even as He prepared Himself for the anguish of the cross.

The Son of God would never have left behind the kind of

disciples He did if He had not opened His life to them. These men were not theologians; they were students of life and stewardship, learning by walking and living with Him. They grew because His life was like Plato's new home—one with a window in every room.

5

When People Show Only One Side

Gail: *I could be wrong, but it looks to me as if you've made five righthand turns in a row. Are you lost?*

Gordon: *No, of course not.*

Gail: *Did you bring the directions?*

Gordon: *Didn't need to. I memorized them. Besides, I know this part of the city.*

Gail: *But we've passed that gas station twice now.*

Gordon: *I got trapped in a right-turn-only lane back there and had to turn around.*

Gail: *So you know exactly where we are?*

Gordon: *No problem. I remember seeing that restaurant before.*

Gail: *Could I make a suggestion? Why don't you stop and ask someone where we are?*

Gordon: *Look, we'll be there in five minutes. I know exactly where we are. (What he was thinking): If I keep driving long enough, we'll find the right street. (What he was subconsciously thinking): Admitting that you're really lost, asking for someone's help, and confessing that you actually forgot the directions is what wimps do.*

We live near a major New York City department store. Its full-length windows disclose magnificent displays of merchandise and in each window is a designer's work of art.

Then there is the back of the building, which faces a dark and somewhat scary alley. On this side, the store's windows and doors are padlocked and painted over. There is extravagant graffiti on the walls; garbage overflows the dumpster. The owners of the department store probably prefer that you not see the back of their building; you're only supposed to look at the windows in the front.

Several years ago, a young man came to visit. Since we had not met before, he filled the first fifteen minutes of our time with an introduction of himself. The first thing he wanted us to know was that he was a graduate of Harvard. He paused after that revelation, apparently waiting for an expression of awe. Not getting such a response, he went on to say that he possessed an exceptional mind and it was only a matter of time before the world awoke to his potential.

Then the subject became "connections," people of his acquaintance who were wealthy and powerful. Among his friends, he said, were presidents and CEOs of many major corporations. Then the subject turned to achievement. He outlined an important theory he had formulated about the stock market and noted the strong possibility that his idea would revolutionize the financial world. This all took place in the first fifteen minutes.

Then we started asking questions, and the questions uncovered an alternative resume: one of a man who was unhappy, disillusioned, failing at his job, struggling with his marriage, and anxious that his performance would never match his potential.

You could say that this man wanted to show us the full-length designer windows in the front of his life. But a few probing questions had taken him into the back alley. Like many, he was frightened of the consequences of what we call transparency, and his instinct was to draw attention to those dimensions of his life that would make him seem valuable and likable.

Transparency is not easy for many of us, especially for men. All through life we develop a habit of keeping feelings, thoughts, dreams, and fears to ourselves. We have the suspicion that if we threw open the windows, there would be ridicule or misunderstanding. It seems easier to keep the windows shut.

So we have to work to get the windows open. You know what happens when you try to open the windows in an old house. Often you discover that they're painted shut and stuck. Some of our windows have been stuck, and we have to get them unstuck.

What are we trying to hide when we resist transparency and show only the good side of our personality? Generally we're trying to hide pain, weakness, or shame. Some of us remember key relationships from which much was expected and little received: an insensitive or emotionally distant parent, a friend who betrayed trust, or a romance that turned sour. Others recall humiliations or failures that scarred the soul. Still others cannot forget times when they tentatively raised the windows of their inner life and received scorn or ridicule from those who didn't know how to handle the information they were trusted with.

Because of such problems in our past, we carefully fashion "front windows" that convey the right impressions and try to draw attention away from our undesirable "back alleys." Our front windows may include an overemphasis on physical beauty, achievement, status, or personality characteristics such as unrelenting humor or biting sarcasm.

If you fill your front windows with enough pleasant items, no one finds the real person inside. Possibly no one will ever find out about your back-alley realities until something out front cracks under stress and you have no choice but to let someone in the back door.

The Imposter Syndrome

In one of his earlier books, Bruce Larson wrote:

> I was driving my motorcycle home from work on a four-lane highway one day. It was rush hour and the traffic was heavy—there was a car behind me, a car in front of me, and a panel truck was passing me on the left. Suddenly a wasp flew into the open front of my shirt. That rascal really began to give it to me with his stinger, *but if you had been passing me at the moment, you wouldn't have known anything was wrong.* Afraid I would panic the whole parade and have an accident, or, even worse, that I would look ridiculous, I continued to ride along looking pleasant and unperturbed. Before I could pull over conveniently and whip off my shirt on a side road, I had six wasp stings (by actual count later that night).
>
> Now all around us today there are people with wasps in their shirts who have chosen to look like Joe or Josephine Cool. They don't want to be embarrassed or to embarrass us, so they miss an opportunity for true community and belonging. (*The Relational Revolution*, Word, 1976.)

Today we are learning that a significant percentage of men and women carry repressed tales of childhood physical and sexual abuse. Others carry past events deep in their memory that occasionally erupt like a geyser of guilt or shame. Because their windows are stuck shut, they are unable to create intimacy or connect with others.

One woman says that she can't appreciate sexual activity with her husband. When he reaches to touch her, her first instinct is to withdraw, to feel revulsion rather than affection. When she fails to respond to him, he begins to feel that he has failed as a lover, and the relationship sinks into further pain because he doubts himself and his capacity to make her happy.

But it is actually the woman who, because of her inability to be transparent, is the cause of the distress. Her struggle is not his fault. At an early age—before their marriage—she had a sexual experience, and now, in moments of sexual embrace, she is reminded of those times. Unable to deal with her guilt before God, herself, or her husband, her guilt remains within and does its corrosive work. Until she can open the window of this room and find forgiveness and healing, her marriage will no doubt bear the stress of unknowability.

There are other cover-ups that make us unknowable, too. We may seek to disguise habits we cannot overcome. We might try to downsize a sense of inferiority in which we perceive ourselves as ignorant, culturally substandard, or simply unable to measure up to what we discern as people's expectations.

We can convince ourselves that almost no one would find us interesting or attractive, should they ever come to know the "real us." We become convinced that self-revelation would draw derision, ostracism, or gossip. All of those fears are liable to be reinforced if, at any time, we fall into a position of extreme vulnerability and some insensitive person exposes our inadequacy and brings us pain.

Now they call this the Impostor Syndrome: the debilitating fear that someone may find us out, that our success, popularity, and reputation are all a sham, a matter of chance, and sooner or later, it will all dissolve and people will discover the real us—incompetent losers.

You probably can remember more than one anguished moment in your life when friends cruelly revealed a secret about you and you became the target of your peer group's laughter. Just a few humiliating experiences of that sort will guarantee increased secrecy, creating a possible pattern of "stuck windows" that could last a lifetime.

Even more serious than avoiding transparency with others is avoiding transparency with ourselves. This is self-deceit. Unable to face some truth about a part of our lives, we choose to suppress it, shading or bricking it over so we don't have to keep facing the pain. The covering over can be done by lying to ourselves, blaming the event upon someone else, or editing the truth into a story that soothes our pride. Before long we will have created a form of personal propaganda that we not only share with others, but come to believe ourselves.

We knew a family who adopted a very young foster child a few years ago. Schooldays came, and it became clear that the boy had some developmental problems that had to be handled. Because of this, school officials decided to hold him back from entering the first grade for one year. His interpretation? "I decided," he told his adoptive parents, "that if I stayed back I could help the teacher, and she really needs the help." At the age of six, he had already mastered the adult game of rewriting history to cover up a perceived failure or shame.

How Can We Become Transparent People?

Elizabeth O'Connor writes:

I heard a story. . . . The central figure was an educated and cultured gentleman. One evening he stayed with two colleagues at his laboratory to work on a project they were all anxious to complete. When they had finished late that night, he invited them to his home for coffee . . . and he fell to sharing with them his interest in Greek architecture. Remembering a new volume that he had on the subject, he took it down from the shelf and handed it to his more advantaged co-worker, who quickly glanced at the pages and returned it to him. He was already putting the book back on the shelf when he glimpsed from the corner of his eye the hand of the other man extended to receive the book. The picture hardly registered. He did not come to terms with what had happened until he was in bed. And then he saw again the hand of the other man reaching to receive the book he had never offered. All unconsciously he had made the judgment that this man, being self-tutored, would not be interested in art. In an automatic way, he had excluded him.

The scientist had not thought himself capable of treating another fellow human like this but *he had enough understanding to know that this was not an isolated incident in his life. It was a glimpse of something in himself of which he was only dimly aware.* He left his bed, and spent the rest of the night sitting in his study reflecting on what had happened. He wanted the picture of it burned in his mind and heart so that it would keep him alert and help him avoid the possibility of his going through life ignoring the outstretched hands of his friends (emphasis added). (*Search for Silence*, Word, 1972.)

In terms of transparency, we will never be able to engage in healthy relationships *until we have labored to know ourselves.* Only when we have pursued a healthy ruthlessness with ourselves can various windows begin to open. What fears, what shames, what disappointments, what guilts, what humiliations mark the back rooms of our lives? Have they been shaded over, painted shut? Even to us? A personal inventory is a necessary beginning.

Both of us practice the discipline of journaling, and what we've discovered is this: The more we journal, the more open we become with people. It is as if seeing who we are on paper seals our frailty in black and white.

C. S. Lewis wrote of this ruthless self-knowledge to an American friend who was tempted to become preoccupied with another person's faults. "Try not to think—much less, speak—of their sins. One's own are a much more profitable theme! And if, on consideration, *one can find no faults on one's own side, then cry for mercy: for this must be a most dangerous delusion*" (emphasis added). (*Letters to an American Lady*, edited by Clyde S. Kilby, Eerdmans, 1967.)

If we wish to enjoy intimacy in our friendships, our families and our marriages, this question of transparency must be examined and managed. How much of ourselves are we willing to reveal to others?

Naturally, you do not open the fullness of your life to everyone, and you make sure that the other party is ready to handle whatever you disclose. John tells us that Jesus did not trust Himself to the Jerusalem crowd, "For he knew their hearts." Knowing their priorities and their motives, Jesus withdrew rather than become totally available and transparent at that moment.

But although there may be some cause for caution, the overly cautious taste a loneliness and solitude that is devastating to the soul.

There are great benefits in transparency. When you pursue transparency, you light up areas of your life that you have never been able to appreciate before, areas of the past, the present, and the future.

From the past you will share an increasing stream of formative experiences: joys and delights, sorrows and hurts. You will appreciate the richness of what formed your friend or spouse, and you will become more sensitive and caring because you have been allowed to see down the corridors of the other's innermost being.

In the present, you will learn about the other's feelings, convictions, concerns, and sense of determination about issues and possibilities.

Regarding the future, you will dream and fantasize together. In such transparency, two marital partners or friends begin to plot the course of their lives together, making sure that the tracks move closer together rather than further apart, converging rather than diverging.

Where there is transparency, there can be enormous growth. As the windows become unshaded, we permit others to offer light to our opinions, our concerns, and our dreams. They help complete our thoughts, balance our extremes, and correct our miscalculations. Our friend or spouse may remind us of parallel situations that we may have forgotten that can bring encouragement, direction, or prevention. But transparency has to happen first.

Brokenness

In spiritual language, transparency could be called brokenness. In the Bible we see great and godly men and women who came to God, transparent and broken. Nehemiah is one of those. Brooding upon the ruins of Jerusalem and seeking a reason for God's lifting His protective hand from the city, Nehemiah concluded, ". . . I and my father's house have sinned. We have acted very corruptly . . ." (Nehemiah 1:6, 7 NAS).

When a person becomes capable of this self-knowledge and is rightly broken before God, he or she has taken the first and perhaps most important step in learning how to be transparent with others.

Gail: *In the early years of our marriage, I found it very hard to be transparent. For example, it was difficult for me to apologize for being wrong.*

Gordon: *That was because you feared being abandoned, wasn't it? Imperfect people get left behind.*

Gail: *You certainly had never communicated that, but I carried that fear into our marriage.*

Gordon: *It took years of reassuring to dissolve that fear, but it did dissolve.*

Gail: *Our marriage would certainly have suffered if we hadn't been able to open the windows together.*

Gordon: *I think we helped each other open the windows. I don't know what I would have done if I hadn't had a wife who made it safe for me to get some of my stuck windows open.*

Gail: *You know, Gordon, if you had wanted to, you could have taken advantage of my fear and manipulated our relationship for your own ends. You encouraged my transparency, and I was able to develop it. As a result, we both grew. It was a key* *lesson in the character development of our children, as well. If we expected them to be transparent with us and later on with others, we had to demonstrate transparency for them in our own lives. It meant admitting when we didn't know answers, when we were wrong and needed to apologize, when we were a bit scared of something, and when we knew there were certain realities in our lives that were bigger than all of us. Our children had to see us as real people; the windows had to be opened.*

Gordon: *We call it the repentant life-style.*

Gail: *I think that, more than anything else, this perspective has made for great strength in our relationship. Any evidence we needed of the truth of this came a few years ago, when the brokenness that comes from repentance brought a great sadness to resolution. And I really believe that a failure followed by a great repentance and transparency can often make a relationship even stronger.*

WITHOUT
SENSITIVITY
The
Heart
Cannot
Be
Touched

6

Sensitivity: The Art of Looking Inside

Gail: *Sometimes we discover the values of intimacy in the craziest of moments.*

Gordon: *What are you thinking about?*

Gail: *I'm thinking of the day when the phone rang and a caller expressed concern about someone who was in the hospital, hoping that a staff member from our church could make a pastoral call.*

Gordon: *That was the time you mixed up some of the information, wasn't it?*

Gail: *I was preoccupied, and I didn't listen closely enough to get the sick person's last name. Then I forgot to ask the room number. What's worse, I was too embarrassed to say to the caller, "I didn't hear the name of the person you're concerned about." In my absentmindedness, I just assumed that our people would know what the call was about.*

Gordon: *Not a good assumption.*

Gail: *What was inportant was your reaction. I felt quite sheepish, and wondered if I should tell you how badly I felt and how sorry I was. There was this temptation to defend myself and make an excuse. Who wants to repent if they're going to be made to feel like a jerk? Your way of handling it was very important.*

Gordon: *You hardly ever make a mistake like that.*

Gail: *That's exactly what you told me the instant I shared the problem with you. You made it easy for me to acknowledge that I'd blown it.*

Gordon: *I saw no reason to treat you badly.*

Gail: *That's the point: You were sensitive to me and knew immediately how embarrassed I was. Your reassurance made it possible for me to admit the truth. It was an example of two values of intimacy merging: You were sensitive, and I was able to be transparent. We later solved the problem of the missing patient, and a pastoral call was made.*

Gordon: *You could say that everybody won!*

Leonard Griffith writes about Dr. Roger Pilkington, an English physician who once journeyed to South Wales to present a series of lectures. Arriving at his hotel much later than he'd expected, he was told by a "tired looking and pale middle-aged receptionist" that only a cold supper would be available. "But if you come into the office any time after nine o'clock you can have a cup of tea," she said.

Later in the evening, after his lecture, Pilkington returned to the hotel and decided to accept the offer of tea. When he appeared at the office, he found the receptionist conversing with several guests. The subject of their discussion was suicide. Pouring him tea, the receptionist invited Pilkington to join the conversation. Soon he found himself the target of questions regarding various methods of suicide and the likeliness of pain associated with each. Some time later, the dreary conversation concluded, the doctor went to his room.

But Griffith writes, Roger Pilkington could not sleep.

He had been lying wide-awake for a few minutes when a feeling came over him which he described as "a sense of being charged like a condenser." Throwing on his dressing gown, he ran down four flights of stairs, walked straight into the inner office, confronted the receptionist, and asked bluntly, "I want to know why you are going to commit suicide." She began to protest, but Dr. Pilkington cut her short. "I know you're going to. I shall not stop you. But you must tell me why you are going to do it."

Persuaded by his intensity, the woman began to tell her story. Her father had once suffered from a disease that caused blindness. Now the receptionist's physician had indicated that her father's disease was hereditary and she would have to prepare herself for the likelihood of a similar experience. She intended suicide, she said, rather than pass through the terrible ordeal she had seen in her father's life.

Pilkington, a specialist in genetics, began to ask numerous questions of the receptionist, and when he had the answers, he concluded that the disease was not, in fact, hereditary. Before long, he had convinced her she had been misinformed.

For this woman who had been living in terror of the future, it was a moment of supreme liberation. Dread, the loss of her love of life, and the intention to end everything had dominated every hour of her thought. Now all of that was neutralized. "You can go back to bed. I know you are not deceiving me," she told him. "Don't worry. I shall not kill myself tonight or ever." (*God in Man's Experience*, Word, 1968.)

What called the doctor from his bed that night and compelled him to confront the receptionist? *Sensitivity.*

Sensitivity: *that unique capacity to see, hear, or feel the realities beneath the surface of people's lives; the ability to determine an appropriate action or response.* Pilkington had been in the room with several others during the conversation, but he was the only one who saw and heard something that propelled him into action. Others had heard the same words; others had enjoyed the same pleasant, if morbid, exchange of information, but only one person sensed there was a deeper agenda hidden beneath the words of the hotel receptionist. He alone seemed able to conclude that another human being needed help. To hear what he heard and do what he did is sensitivity.

The Sensitivity of Jesus

Several chapters ago, we started with Jesus' command to the disciples to love one another. It was a brand of unprecedented love, He said, that should be modeled after the way He had loved them. When we study the life of the Lord and His love for His disciples, we see that Jesus was a master of sensitivity. His capacity to look into people and discern true need and true evil was unparalleled. As John put it when Jesus turned away from the crowd that sought to promote Him as their political savior, "he knew what was in them."

No one seems to have profited more from the sensitivity of Jesus than His friend Simon Peter. Take one of the earliest recorded encounters between the two, when Peter fell on his knees before Christ. Peter was probably intimidated by what he perceived to be the awesome power and capacity of Jesus. "Go away from me, Lord," he babbled, "I am a sinful man!" But the sensitive Christ knew better than to trust Peter's words. Jesus knew fear in a man when He saw it, and He was able to calm the fisherman. "Peter, don't be afraid," the Lord told him; "you're going to become a 'fisher' of men." Thus began a remarkable and intimate friendship, begun with sensitivity!

Jesus was insightful enough to know when the disciples were confused about the nature of greatness and penetrated their silence to pull their perplexities to the surface. He was discerning about the protests of faithfulness the twelve made, knowing that they were unprepared to keep those promises. Rather than accept their intentions of loyalty, He made it quite plain, especially to Peter, that He fully understood their weaknesses and was praying for their responses in their hours of deepest stress.

Jesus seemed to be one step ahead of everyone else, because He saw what virtually no one else saw. He didn't need to wait for a person's words, nor did He have to pry and poke about. He just knew. Jesus was the most sensitive person who ever walked the earth.

What Is Sensitivity?

On a physiological level, sensitivity is the ability to make judgments about something through touch, taste, sight, sound, or smell. When these five senses are fully operative, they provide enormous amounts of information to you.

We once spent a day in an up-country West African village where people who suffered from Hanson's Disease (once known as leprosy) lived. While there, we learned that people with this disease often lose fingers, toes, or other extremities because they are no longer able to sense pain, due to insensitive nerve endings. Unable to perceive heat, they are liable to burn their fingers over a fire. Not feeling the bite of a spider, they are ignorant of the fact that poison has been injected into their bloodstream. Sometimes unaware that they have cut themselves, they are not prepared for the possibility of infection. Physiologically speaking, they are not sensitive people.

When you enter into a relationship with your relational nerve endings damaged, undeveloped, or simply inoperative, you are apt to face lots of problems: conflicts in which words cut and immobilize, feelings of neglect, and the perception that you are not understood or appreciated.

Insensitive people remain unaware of how their actions or words impact another person. They cannot or do not read the signals that reflect dismay in another. They do not know how to reassure with words or gestures that bring peace. They forget the importance of symbols and events such as birthdays, anniversaries, gifts, and past memories. They can be abrupt in their candor, unhearing when it comes to others' requests and expectations. Satisfying intimacy is out of the question for an insensitive person.

Sensitivity in the Garden

Biblically speaking, the issue of sensitivity has its roots in the Garden of Eden. When Adam chose to violate the law of God and lost his transparency, the effect was immediate and tragic. Eve could no longer enjoy the natural intimacy of fully knowing Adam. The windows and doors of Adam's life were nailed shut, so how could Eve know what was going on inside her husband? What was he thinking, feeling, struggling with, wondering about? How could she know?

Eve now had to depend upon what Adam told her about himself. She had to listen to and weigh his words. She had to watch his face and body language. As she worked at this, she had to pay as much attention to what he didn't say or do as to what he did.

No matter how good Eve became at deciphering Adam's true feelings, she could only look within him to a certain degree. If she was to know him intimately, he would have to work at being transparent. A "cooperation of relationship" was necessary. He had to be transparent; she had to be sensitive. To the extent that they worked hard on this, the truth about each other could be known, and intimacy would occur.

For instance, a daughter, now an adult, approached her mother with a very important issue concerning her future. She loved her mother dearly and was committed to her mother's authority because of their particular cultural background.

The daughter had thought about this conversation for weeks, even prayed that somehow her mother would understand the decision she wanted to make. She had rehearsed her conversation with great care.

As soon as the daughter began to speak, her mother exploded with anger and threatened a break in the family relationship if the daughter persisted with her ideas. As a result, the daughter abandoned the conversation.

It could have been a great moment of intimacy between mother and daughter, if the mother had realized she was a captive of her own fears that the traditional family ways might be violated and the family shamed. If she could have been sensitive to her daughter's respect, the conversation might have gone on to a mutually beneficial solution. Sensitivity on the mother's part would have also provided room for the daughter to be transparent, and the two could have resolved the issue together. But the mother's lack of sensitivity devastated any attempt at transparency and damaged the intimacy between them.

Gender and Sensitivity

For the most part, women tend to be more sensitive than men; this has been demonstrated in many research projects.

In her book *Unfinished Business* (Ballantine, 1980), Maggie Scarf notes a study done at Yale University on the subject of depression among college students. "When females were depressed," writes Scarf, "they suffered 'significantly higher levels of . . . experiences of loneliness, helplessness, dependency and the need for external sources of security.' But, in contrast, for males, depression had to do much more with 'self criticism and the failure to live up to expectation.' "

Women, Scarf concluded, become depressed about the insufficiency of their relationships, whereas men tend to become depressed about their failure to achieve, to "make it, to gain control of and mastery over the environment."

Because they are much more concerned about the health of their relationships than men are, women are liable to be more sensitive to what makes relationships work and what is causing a relationship to falter. Women are more likely to do the first listening, the first watching; and the first to read the signals beneath the surface.

Many men, on the other hand, ignore the importance of doing this. They give way to their stronger desire to achieve and accumulate things. As a result, they are negligent in determining what might be wrong in a relationship until it is almost too late to do anything about it. Only when trouble is obvious and unavoidable are many men willing to act.

Often wives come to us seeking help for their deteriorating marriages. Their husbands show little or no inclination to ask for help. Only when the wife decides to leave home does she gain her husband's attention. Then he realizes the seriousness of the situation and comes rushing to the counselor or therapist, ready to make any change, go to any extreme to revive the marriage. But by then it is often too late. What happened? He never really took the time to explore his wife's inner world. He lacked sensitivity.

Just being female does not make a person sensitive. Many women are extremely insensitive. They may be too concerned about themselves to spend the time it takes to penetrate another's world.

Imagine a widow and widower who have decided to marry. The daughter of the widower has refused to give her blessing to the marriage because all she can think about is the intrusion the new wife will be upon her relationship with her father. She will lose her special intimacy with him, she thinks; she will probably have to move out of his home; she will have to face the fact that another woman is going to influence her father. Since the marriage threatens her, she is against it. It does not occur to her that her father is terribly lonely and has found someone with whom he can share marital love. She has not taken the time to sense his needs because she is too consumed with her own.

Some people never sharpen their capacity for sensitivity because they don't need to. They so dominate their worlds and the people in them that they worry little about understanding anyone but themselves. If one enjoys extreme personal attractiveness, easily acquired wealth, unusual natural charisma, or even great physical size, there may be a tendency for others to defer to them. Always being the dominant person, the one in control, they lose their ability to wonder what anyone else thinks or cares about. The result can be one who easily offends, leaves hurt behind them, causes inconvenience to others—and never knows it!

This issue of sensitivity became one of the most important things in our pursuit of intimacy in marriage.

Gail: *Sometimes there may be a conflict of sensitivities that can crowd out the needs of those we love.*

Gordon: *What do you mean?*

Gail: *Well, when I became a believer, my longing for my family to understand my newfound joy superseded my sensitivity to how my new faith would affect them. I was like a bull in a china shop—bold, judgmental, eager, insistent. My parents gave me* *a religious upbringing, and in my eagerness, I was giving them the message that they had failed me. I should have been building on what they had given me, appreciating what we shared in common.*

Gordon: *Eventually your folks did come to appreciate your faith.*

Gail: *Yes, but only after I learned to stay away from controversy, to serve, and to emphasize things we had in common.*

Gordon: *You have certainly become a very sensitive person, Gail. At times, you can look into my eyes and know exactly what I'm thinking. I find it very difficult to keep a secret from you.*

Gail: *Sometimes, I think I can see right through you. Before sin entered the world, I'm sure Eve could look through Adam a lot better than I can look through you. The truth is that, when I look at you, all I can do is make some educated guesses.*

Gordon: *And, I must admit, you do it rather well.*

7
Waiting for a Good Moment

Gordon: *You've given me a wonderful gift.*

Gail: *What are you thinking of?*

Gordon: *You gave me the gift of sensitivity. It may sound kind of foolish, but before I knew you, I never realized how much someone could discern in other people. Time and time again you would see things in the eyes, the gestures, or the body language of people that tipped you off to something that was otherwise hidden. You not only saw things, you heard things in the way people talked that gave you a chance to be a better friend or carer. I admired that.*

Gail: *Weren't there a few times when it got on your nerves?*

Gordon: *I suppose. Some of the times when we were coming home from a party or a group meeting, you'd start telling me about how this or that person was really feeling. What intrigued me was that you were right. I'd go back a day later and discover that you had that person pegged.*

Gail: *I've always had an awareness that most of us conceal things, sometimes intentionally, sometimes not. We hide our pain, fear, hopes, and resentments. Good friends look for those kinds of things and try to give encouragement or become a sounding board.*

Gordon: *Sometimes it was unnerving to me to realize how far*

> *ahead you were in things like this. But I decided if you could do it, I might be able to learn something about it, so I tried watching the way I knew you were watching.*

Gail: *You sharpened your sensitivity pretty quickly.*

Gordon: *I came to realize that there are all sorts of levels in human experience that you can appreciate, if you concentrate on being sensitive. You spot the signs of hostility, or know who feels intimidated or wishes they weren't there. You learn that some people are dying to get a word into the conversation but can't compete with the faster talkers. And you begin to see who needs encouragement and appreciation. It's all there, but some of us have to learn to spot it and understand what to do with the information.*

Gail: *You've done well at both. You're good evidence that sensitivity can be learned—even late in life.*

Anyone who takes the pursuit of sensitivity seriously will, sooner or later, have to take a hard look at Jesus, the most sensitive person who ever lived. This quality showed itself forcefully when He hung on the cross, nearing death.

There He was, sensitive to the evil that possessed the crowd. Knowing their greatest need, He prayed for them: "Father forgive them; for they do not know what they are doing" (Luke 23:34 NAS).

He was also sensitive to the dying thief at His side who cried out for hope. To him He said: "Today you shall be with Me in Paradise" (Luke 23:43 NAS). Then in a beautiful and tender moment, Jesus asserted His strong concern for the welfare of His mother. He made sure that John would care for her. "Here is your mother," He said (John 19:27 NIV). All of this went on while He agonized in His own coming death. This is sensitivity under great stress at a time when we would be inclined to care only for ourselves. Jesus always saw, heard, and tied into the most important issues—things usually forgotten, neglected, or simply unseen by others.

Sensitivity means an "ear" is at work. It hears the music that surrounds words. It takes note of what isn't being said, of silences, of unuttered groans and sighs. It carefully observes eyes and facial expressions for unspoken clues. Sensitivity picks up on such things as fatigue, unhappiness, expectation, loneliness, or hurt.

E. Stanley Jones writes:

> You can judge how far you have risen in the scale of life by asking one question: How wisely do I and how deeply do I care? . . . To be Christianized is to be sensitized: Christians are people who care. No one, anywhere, can come into authentic contact with Jesus Christ in personal surrender and obedience without beginning to care. It was the first reaction I felt when I arose from my knees in the hour of conversion. I felt as though I wanted to put my arms around the world and share this with everybody. (*A Song of Ascents*, Abingdon, 1979.)

God means for us to have the kind of inner "receptors" that make it possible to hear the silent messages another in your circle of intimacy may be sending. And we believe God wants us to pursue sensitivity, for it is the gateway to the kind of caring necessary in intimacy. When we look about us, we can see sensitivity working in all sorts of situations, to everyone's gain.

In Hawaii we met a lay leader named Ike, who had grown up as a Buddhist. His children were drawn to life at a local Protestant church, so Ike drove them to Sunday school each week. Sometimes he would go off and leave them at the front door and return at the end of the morning, but it was not unusual for him to sit on the front steps of the church for a long while, waiting for the conclusion of Sunday school.

A woman in the church named Ruth had a unique way of making people feel welcome and appreciated. Ruth made orchid leis and brought them to church each week, asking God to help her choose those visitors who would benefit most from such a gift.

Ruth took note of Ike's routine, and one day when he was sitting by himself she walked up and presented him with a beautiful orchid lei. It was the perfect thing to make a lonely man feel accepted, and it drew him into the building, where he heard the gospel and later chose to follow Christ.

How Do You Learn Sensitivity?

How is sensitivity developed? We've been asked that question many times, and it is tempting to answer: "You just have it," because it does come naturally to many. But many people simply do not have it. It's not a natural part of their personality.

So how is it learned? How do you start?

1. We might start by praying for it! Sensitivity is in part a gift of God's Spirit. Make this gift a matter of prayer, asking God for an enlivening of the hunches, promptings, and proddings that often arise out of the heart and emotions.

But this means we must respond to those nudges from within, when they come. We must give when the message comes to be generous; encourage when the prodding comes that someone needs lifting and appreciation; listen when the hunch says that this is a person in need of a kind ear; ask questions when the signal says that a person needs to be drawn out of himself and into conversation.

Jesus wants His people to be sensitive, but sensitivity is given through prayer, a listening heart, and careful, consistent practice.

2. Study sensitivity as a theme in the Bible, in the lives of great saints, and in mature people you know. If one develops curiosity about the way they respond to situations, the things they listen and look for, the conclusion to which they come when they are dealing with people, you will learn fast. It's important to ask sensitive people how they have come to be discerning.

A close friend of ours—a very sensitive man—is a physician. Once he told us how important it was to make a visit to a patient just before he or she went into surgery. He was aware that all surgical patients have tremendous anxieties. Will something go wrong? Will they come out of the anesthetic? He had come to realize the importance of speaking to those fears by giving a word of hope.

"I always make sure that I review the surgical procedure once more with them, and then I conclude by saying this to them: 'When you are in the recovery room and begin to wake up, I will come in and see you and tell you how everything went.'" The reassurance that he would be coming to see them helped put the worst of their fears to rest. His word of hope brought peace to troubled minds. That is sensitivity.

3. Do what a friend calls "watch life in the streets, and ask a lot of questions." She got the idea, she says, from Solomon, who observed that object lessons are everywhere, teaching us how people feel and what they need.

One day our friend was waiting her turn in a long checkout line. Customers were hostile and aggressive, and the cashier began to take more than a little verbal abuse from those who wanted to vent their frustrations. But the clerk seemed unflappable.

When asked how she could remain so calm in the midst of such mistreatment, the clerk responded, "Well, I've got eight children at home. And I learned a long time ago not to sweat the small stuff.''

It was a short encounter, but our friend, sensitive to the mature response of a person under fire, asked a question and gained an insightful answer that could be absorbed into anyone's life by watching, asking questions, and thinking through the value of the answers. Sensitivity comes as we study others and ask ourselves what makes them who they are.

We were eating lunch one day with a husband and wife whom we dearly love and admire. They were both in their eighties. We were impressed with the vitality of their relationship, their affection and endearing words for each other.

"Do the two of you ever have conflicts?" we asked.

"Oh, sure," the husband said. "But I have to be careful to make sure that if I disagree with her or want to correct her, I wait for the right moment. So I simply say, 'When you have a good moment, I have a thought for you.' ''

"Why would you say it that way?"

The husband answered, "I learned a long time ago that she was bruised by an insensitive father who said very cruel things to her when she was a child. It made her feel terribly insecure."

"Are you saying that hurt feelings and insecurity from childhood can still prevail when men and women are in their eighties?" we asked.

"Yes, I'm saying that," he responded. "We never outgrow some of those things. When I say something disagreeable, I don't want to do it in such a way that causes memory of that early pain, so I wait for a good moment."

When Jesus talked with the disciples concerning His coming execution in Jerusalem, Scripture says, "They did not understand the saying, and they were afraid to ask him." The failure of the twelve to look into things and ask questions when they had the chance is a key to their pathetic response on the night of Jesus' arrest.

Their failure to question also points up their insensitivity to Christ. If they had thought through what He was saying, they might have cared for Him far more tenderly and been more of a friend to Him in His lonely, suffering hours. But they weren't sensitive enough to ask the defining questions, so they remained conscious only of the surface events, when they should have been developing discernment.

4. Sensitivity is learned when we "sit where they sit." Those words are from the early part of the Book of Ezekiel, where God challenges the young prophet to become aware of the needs of the suffering people about him. When he did go and sit where they sat and remained for seven days, Ezekiel was overwhelmed by the reality of their situation.

Sensitive people understand that difficult moments in life are inevitable. They are prepared to detect those moments, identify with them, and share the pain. They do their best to acknowledge feelings, pains, predicaments, and consequences, and they always bring along a word of hope and grace. The more it's practiced, the more sensitive one becomes.

We remember a conversation with a friend who was struggling with cancer. We asked if his pastor was an encouragement to him. He answered, "Frankly, I kind of hate to see our pastor come around. He spends all his time telling me how I *ought* to feel. He never asks how I actually do feel or offers me a chance to be honest about my emotions or doubts. I end up feeling guilty that I'm not quite the kind of person he thinks I ought to be."

We also recall a valued couple who faced the divorce of one of their children. They were shocked at how few people could speak to them about the situation. At first they felt rejected, but because of their maturity, they eventually realized that most people simply didn't know what to say, so they said nothing. Later, they told us that people in relational pain do not need answers, only a touch, a reminder that friends are praying, caring, and still love them. Only those who had gone through similar experiences knew what to say to them—those who had sat where they sat.

5. We proactively open our ears and eyes. The sensitive person says, "I will treat people the way they need to be treated, not the way I want to treat them."

"Hello! Is there anyone out there who will listen to me? How can I convince you that I am a prisoner? For the past five years I have not seen a park or the ocean or even just a few feet of grass." So writes an eighty-four-year-old woman from a nursing home. She has been neglected and abused.

> Most of the nurses' aides who work here are from other countries. Even those who can speak English don't have much in common with us. So they hurry to get their work done as quickly as possible. There are a few caring people who work here, but there are so many of us who are needy for that kind of honest attention.
>
> A doctor comes to see me once a month. He spends approximately three to five seconds with me and then a few more minutes writing in the chart or joking with the nurses. . . . I sometimes wonder about how the nurses' aides feel when they work so hard for so little money and then see that the person who spends so little time is the one who is paid the most.

This is a person crying to be heard, and no one appears to be listening. She is one of millions whose voices are not being heard.

I am writing this because many of you may live to be old like me, and by then it will be too late. You, too, will be stuck here and wonder why nothing is being done, and you, too, will wonder if there is any justice in life. Right now I pray every night that I may die in my sleep and get this nightmare of what someone has called life over with, if it means living in this prison day after day. (*Hartford Courant*, October 5, 1979.)

All around us are many who need that touch and that attentive ear and eye. Frequently we miss them because we are too busy doing other things. It's not just in nursing homes. It's in apartments and homes where single mothers share living accommodations. It's in our own families, where we are becoming too rushed to practice sensitivity toward one another. And in the office, where life is being pursued at such a high pitch that it seems to be impossible to take time to listen.

But when we open our eyes and our ears to watch and listen, we not only search for "felt" needs but also for people's vulnerabilities. Some people need our protection; others need us to back off; still others need a sounding board, not pat answers.

In *The Celebration of Discipline* (Harper & Row, 1978), Richard Foster tells of a debate that took place between George Fox and Nathaniel Stephens. Fox, with his incredible mind, quickly and insensitively overwhelmed Stephens, almost to the point of humiliation. Stephens said, "Mr. Fox, I fear your sun-light has blocked out my starlight." Fox had something to learn about sensitivity.

In healthy relationships we learn to ask the question: What does this person need that I can give? A father learns when his son needs an encouraging word or a rebuke. He learns when his daughter needs affection and when she needs a male figure who believes in her capabilities as a person. A woman learns when her husband needs to be left alone and when he needs her resourceful presence. A mentor learns when the disciple needs a quick answer and when he needs to discover it for himself. In so doing, they are expressing sensitivity.

Catherine Booth, cofounder of the Salvation Army, was a remarkably sensitive person. Her discernment showed best in her relationship with William, her husband. In a letter to him, she declared her intent that their home would always be a place sensitive to his needs and concerns:

> I am delighted; it makes me happy to hear you speak as you do about home. Yes, if you will seek home, love home, be happy at home, I will spend my energies in trying to make it a more than ordinary one; it shall, if my ability can do it, be a spot sunny and bright, pure and calm, refined and tender, a fit school in which to train immortal spirits for a holy and glorious heaven; a fit resting-place for a spirit pressed and anxious about public duties; but oh, I know it is easy to talk, I feel how liable I am to fall short; but it is well to purpose right, to aim high, to hope much; yes, we will make home for each other the brightest spot on earth, we will be tender, thoughtful, loving, and forbearing, will we not? Yes, we will. (Quoted in *Life of General William Booth* by Harold Begbie, Macmillan, 1920.)

These are the words of a woman who had looked within a man and found something she could give. Intimacy drips from that page.

It was sensitivity that caused Roger Pilkington to perceive the anguish of a lonely, frightened hotel receptionist and direct her away from suicide. It was sensitivity that we had to learn and keep on trying to learn if we were to achieve the intimacy we so strongly believe in.

Gail: *When our children were babies, we used to speak of something called the "mother's ear." As long as I was nursing our tiny ones, my ear seemed to pick up the slightest stir in the cradle. For some unexplained reason, my mother's ear deserted me soon after I finished the nursing phase.*

Gordon: *And then I was the one who could hear the slightest sound. That's a good illustration of the kind of sensitivity we need to develop.*

Gail: *It's a matter of development, of working on it, of obeying the inner prompting. Recently the name of a friend kept coming to my mind, so I phoned her and told her I had been thinking of her. She was so grateful for the call, because only a few hours earlier she had rushed her father to the hospital with congestive heart failure.*

Gordon: *We often miss such opportunities by not listening and not caring enough to follow through.*

Gail: *I remember when a man stepped to the front of the sanctuary in a church of ours and recalled how he had responded earlier to your public invitation. That was the first time in months that anyone had physically touched him, looked him in the eye, and given him undivided attention for five minutes.*

Gordon: *Yes, I remember the time. I never realized how much it had meant to him until he told me about it later.*

WITHOUT
COMMUNICATION
The
Heart
Cannot
Be
Touched

parently Mahler's capacity to relate to others left something to be desired. His life was marked with examples of how *not* to win friends and influence people.

Noted symphony conductor Bruno Walter, who wrote Mahler's biography, tells of a hot June day when a hopeful young composer came to the maestro's studio, hoping to gain Mahler's endorsement of a newly written opera. Walter left the two alone to examine the score at the keyboard and returned some time later. Judging from Walter's description, the opera was a bomb. The problem was that Mahler had no idea how to handle such a delicate moment, no conception of how to protect the young man from total disappointment.

> I joined them toward the end of the last scene and found them in their shirt-sleeves, the composer perspiring profusely and Mahler obviously sunk in the depths of boredom and aversion. When the playing had ended, Mahler did not utter a word. The composer, too, probably deeply hurt by Mahler's silence, said nothing, and I saw no chance of saving the awkward situation by any effort of my own. There was no help for it: the composer put on his coat, wrapped up his score, and after a silence that lasted for several minutes and a coldly polite, "*Auf wiedersehen*" terminated the painful scene. *An entire life time of personal relations of all kinds had not supplied Mahler with that modicum of social polish that would have brought the meeting to an ordinary end* (emphasis ours). (*Themes and Variations: An Autobiography*, translated by James Gulston, Knopf, 1946.)

A perceptive man could have saved the feelings of the aspiring composer by knowing what to say and how to say it, but Mahler, the writer of magnificent music, was not a communicator. As a result, a young person desperate for approval and

8
The Gift of Talking

Gordon: *You know, when I was in high school and college, I dated a lot of girls.*

Gail: *You have to remind me of that?*

Gordon: *No, that wasn't the point. What I wanted to say is tha[t] you were the first person I met that I could connect with All the others didn't seem to value the things that w[ere] important to me. You were different.*

Gail: *How so?*

Gordon: *Every time we got talking about an idea or a dream [or] opinion, you'd dive into the conversation with [such] enthusiasm. You usually assured me that there was [some]thing significant in what I was saying.*

Gail: *I enjoyed asking questions and adding to your though[ts so I] could polish them into something even better.*

Gordon: *Suddenly you had me talking about feelings, e[xciting] dreams, and even hurts that I didn't know an[yone would] ever be interested in. I'd go home after an e[vening with] you, exhilarated because I'd been heard.*

Gail: *So that's why you married me.*

Gordon: *Let's just say it was no small part of the r[eason].*

Gustav Mahler was a brilliant musician and c[omposer, but] expertise in one area does not guarantee skill i[n] encouragement from another whose judgment counted for something was left angry, empty, and humiliated.

Perhaps the simplest and yet the most difficult thing for many people to do in a relationship is to talk in such a way that everyone leaves fulfilled and whole.

Jesus the Communicator

How did Christ love the men who followed most closely after Him? *He communicated with them* in a score of ways. He told them stories; He answered endless questions; He gave directives about life; He opened up the mysteries of Scripture; He disclosed His expectations about the future. When necessary, He said the hard thing, but even His tough words were enveloped in care.

On the other hand, He was a listener, responding to their anxieties and concerns. He watched them carefully and knew the intent of their hearts and minds at every moment. Jesus not only extended Himself toward people, He connected in every possible way.

If there was doubt in a man's voice or actions, Jesus was gentle with the weakness but firm in bringing the doubter face-to-face with the truth. If others misjudged the motives of a well-meaning person, Jesus was quick to sort out the issues and remove the confusion. Wherever Christ was, there was sure to be maximum light on the moment, because Jesus was a communicator; He made sure everyone was in full possession of the facts.

To communicate, you must be able to name, to own (without embarrassment), and to express feelings, judgments, and convictions while assuming that they will be heard and accepted without ridicule or retribution. Many relationships suffer from a lack of communication because of ridicule and retribution. That was the experience of the young man who visited Mahler.

A corporation president told us of an executive in his firm who had to be dismissed. "He was a brilliant man," our friend said, "but the fact was that he couldn't get along with anybody. You never really knew what he was thinking, and he wasn't about to tell you. He became a liability rather than an asset. He simply had to go."

How Do We Communicate?

There are many ways to communicate beyond words. We can discern what another is thinking, for example, by noting body language: the use of hands, gestures, or posture.

We communicate with our faces, through frowns, smiles, and the expression in our eyes. We even communicate through our personal odors. We are likely sending messages when we choose to take time to be clean, groomed, and scented in ways that seem pleasing to others in our culture.

We also communicate by the way we use space. Depending on how we feel about a person, we may draw closer or farther away. You can always spot lovers from a distance by their proximity to each other.

When a couple comes to our home to discuss a problem, we can often gauge the severity of their hostile feelings for each other by where they choose to sit. One couple sat at the extreme ends of the sofa. I doubt they were even aware of the message they were sending. It was fun for us to watch them sit closer and closer on the sofa as their relationship healed.

Some people appear to be sending messages about their state of mind and soul by where they sit in church. If they feel in touch with God, you may find them seated somewhere near the front, where the action is likely to be. They want as little as possible to distract them from hearing and participating. But if they are feeling spiritually cold or even rebellious, they may find a seat in the back of the sanctuary or up in the balcony, and when the service is concluded, they will avoid the door where the pastor is greeting people. Somehow they equate shaking hands with the pastor with having to come to terms with God.

When someone speaks, we listen for the tone of voice, volume, and speed of speaking, and we listen for silence— what is being said and what is not being said. It's when you listen for silence that you are liable to hear the most important messages.

You learn to look for signs in behavior that are out of the ordinary in terms of the person's normal responses. Once we noticed that an acquaintance was dressed totally out of line with his regular habits. Usually he wouldn't be caught dead without every article of clothing color coordinated, but on this occasion, he had mixed plaids and stripes, and his colors clashed terribly. For many people, that wouldn't and shouldn't mean a thing, but not for this man. A closer look revealed tired eyes and a sagging posture. When we began to probe, he instantly poured out his heart about a terrible humiliation he was facing.

Some people seem to be playing a game with you. They almost challenge you to find out what is really going on inside them. We have often watched people in severe anxiety smile and offer the glad hand to anyone they meet. But if you were to ask them specifically about their personal relationships they will dissolve into tears. That's one reason we have felt it even more important to seek out the hidden messages people are inadvertently delivering. They would deny it, but they are usually hoping that someone picks up their code and bothers to ask. Even a person's unwillingness to meet another's eye has a revealing tale to tell. The eyes are usually the mirrors of the soul. You can read shame, hurt, or joy in someone's eyes if you are concerned enough to learn how to read them.

And, of course, we communicate with words. The choice of those words is very important. Words can cut like a knife, soothe like a tender caress, enthuse, discourage, open up mysteries, and make a weak person strong.

When Communication Is Stifled

On the other hand, communication can be deliberately squelched when people, by choice or neglect, create an atmosphere in which communication and intimacy become impossible. That happens in homes and offices all the time.

The oldest son of singer Bing Crosby, Gary, wrote of the breakdown of his relationship with his father and pinned it all on their inability to communicate. Professionally, Bing Crosby was a remarkable communicator, but in his home, his son writes, he was unable to express love or joy for his children in a way they could understand. As a result, everyone in the family suffered. (*Going My Way* by Gary Crosby with Ross Firestone, Doubleday, 1983.)

Communication can be a problem for many reasons. Sometimes it may be because of lack of time, conflicting schedules, and pressure. A century ago, when most families worked together day and night, there was a common language, a common task, and a common need for talk of all kinds. Today that need has been seriously impaired. In too many homes, family talking skills are undeveloped. Instead of working at talking, which in fact must be done, too many families make the easy choice to live vicariously through TV sitcoms, where talking looks easy.

Sometimes communication in relationships does not happen because people have nothing of value to say. Having come from a family background where their words were generally ridiculed, they have developed the habit of not saying anything that might bring them ridicule, argument, or competition. They keep their feelings, opinions, and concerns to themselves, and only the most intensive questioning (which can backfire) will elicit any self-revelation.

In many relationships communication slackens because one of the parties has learned that the other will challenge anything that is said. One person may not accept criticism; another will not allow an observation to pass without trying to improve it. Thus communication degenerates, simply because everything seems to end up in confrontation. Before long, the other party in the relationship resorts to silence.

We will not communicate with a person who squelches everything we say; nor will we communicate when our words are likely to be used against us in the future or revealed to someone else.

Sometimes communication breaks down because of a lack of understanding on the part of the hearer. The disciples often had this kind of problem. Jesus would tell them things about Himself, about the future, about their own potential, and they simply couldn't bring themselves to internalize what He told them.

When Jesus was about to ascend to heaven, He told them, "You don't understand what I'm saying now, but some day you will." They lacked faith at times; they had contradicting personal interests at other times. Sometimes they were engulfed in fear; on other occasions they were too culturally conditioned to think of the possibilities Christ was offering them.

Certain issues in life—those to which a person attaches emotional significance—may never get a fair hearing, no matter how clear and plain the speaker may be.

Enhancing Our Conversations

In the fine writings of John Powell (*The Secret of Staying in Love*, Tabor, 1990), we discovered a marvelous tool to measure the quality of our conversation. He pointed out that there are five levels of verbal communication, each quite necessary to the pursuit of intimacy but each a bit more profound than the preceding one.

We latched on to this simple structure of conversation, taught it to our children when they were younger, and then later found it helpful in aiding people who come to us for help in the matter of communication.

Level One

To begin with, Powell wrote about something he called the level of cliché. Clichés are the most common of all verbal and nonverbal ways by which people connect. Clichés are more or less exchanges of meaningful symbols; we call them verbal algebra. Grunts, a word or two, a simple sentence can be clichés. A handshake, for example, is a cliché in gesture form. It suggests an extension of friendship or greeting and proposes that nothing of hostile intent exists between two people.

That notion got us to thinking about famous handshakes and, in some cases, famous "unhandshakes." In 1954, Chou En-lai, then premier of the People's Republic of China, went to Geneva to represent his government at a conference on the future of Indochina. Entering the conference room a few minutes before the meeting was to begin, he spied John Foster Dulles, the American secretary of state, and went to greet him.

When Chou extended his hand, Dulles drew back, putting his own hand behind his back, publicly snubbing the Communist. It was a humiliating moment for Chou En-lai, and he never forgot what happened. Historians have speculated that that bit of hostile level-one communication—on a diplomatic cliché level—created the momentum that kept the Chinese and American governments out of touch for almost two decades. Years later, when there was need for high-level diplomatic contact to settle the conflict in Vietnam, there was no common ground for conversation between the United States and China. Could thousands have died because at a key moment in history one man could not respond to the level-one gesture of another?

People often send level-one signals to one another which then set the pace for the future of the relationship. A level-one signal that is read as positive can be the cause of a subsequent romance, the proposal of a business negotiation, or the feeling that one is welcomed in a social setting. But a level-one signal read as negative can be the beginning of defensiveness, avoidance, or retaliation in a discussion.

We use verbal clichés all the time, of course, with good reason. Meet a friend in the corridor at work when there is not time to visit, and you may say in passing, "How're you doing?" The other responds, "Not bad. How's yourself?" "Super!" comes the reply. Perhaps both add a concluding "Have a good day!" as they walk away.

What's been said in that communication? Not a whole lot, really. At best, the two people know that each is generally all right (but not necessarily), that they are on speaking terms, and that they're equally busy and now is not a time to talk. All that and more can be contained in clichés. And that may have been all that was necessary or important to say at that moment.

Clichés are, in fact, a necessary part of a busy culture. We wouldn't have time to say all the things we'd like to say if we didn't use clichés.

We once spent some time in a country where Islam was the prevailing religion. The missionaries who were our hosts related how time-consuming it was to go to market, because every person they knew would stop and engage them in endless conversation, formal greetings, questions and answers, all of which were part of their way of life. "How's your mother, your father, your sisters, your brothers? How are the people in your village?" These questions were not only asked, but it was expected that they would be reciprocated. Much of their marketing time, the missionaries told us, was taken up in simply greeting people. Fortunately or unfortunately, rightly or wrongly, for the best reasons or the worst, in our culture, we save time by reducing those exchanges to clichés. Our level-one signals shorten these conversations to a matter of seconds. "Hi!" "Nice to see ya!" "Hey, man!" "Yo!"

Obviously there is nothing wrong with clichés in their place. But if the cliché is the only level of communication at which two people operate, something is seriously lacking. Intimacy is never sustained on level one. It isn't even born there.

Sometimes well-meaning Christians will operate at the cliché level with their friends. Afraid to get beneath the surface to where people really think and feel, conversations are reduced to a religious formula that can be quite meaningless. Think of some of the things we unthinkingly say to each other.

"Be praying for you, brother." The expression may mean just that. On the other hand, it might suggest that is *all* we intend to do for that person, and they should not expect anything more. Do you remember Linus standing in front of Snoopy's doghouse in the middle of a raging blizzard, exhorting a freezing Snoopy, "Be warmed, Snoopy. Be of good cheer and be warmed!" Snoopy would have much preferred to have been invited into Linus's house and given a warm bowl of food.

Occasionally we have taught John Powell's levels of conversation to various groups of people. When we've done so, we've used sample conversations to illustrate each of the levels. Although it's difficult to simulate a thoroughly natural conversation, we've used some tongue-in-cheek dialogues such as the following to help people hear themselves when clichés are the order of the day. In this conversation, we're actors. Frankly, we are always impressed by the laughter from the audiences. It tells us that this sort of talk may happen more than anyone realizes.

Woman: *Good morning. Isn't it a terrific day? I can't believe we've got a whole day to ourselves. No place to go; no people to meet; no problems to solve. And I feel so terrific. When was the last time we had a day like that?*

Man: *Umm.*

Woman: *Did you sleep well? It seemed like you were gone the moment you hit the pillow.*

Man: *Something like that.*

Woman: *Well, how do you feel after a week's work like this last one? You put in an awful lot of hours. You must really be ready to crash.*

Man: *Oh, you know . . .*

Woman: *I just died last night. I worked so hard to get things back into order after finishing that article I've been working on. It seemed I had papers all over the house. I wanted so hard for things to be orderly when you got home from your trip to California. I know how much you appreciate coming home to a peaceful place.*

Man: *Yep.*

Woman: *Did you notice that I hung that picture that you asked me to frame? I sensed that it was important to you to get that up before the Briggs come over next week. But you haven't said anything about it.*

Man: *It's nice.*

Woman: *Nice? Is that all you have to say about it? I thought you'd be thrilled.*

Man: *Yeah, I guess I was.*

Woman: *Something bothering you? Was the California trip as good as you thought it might be? Or is there something about it that you haven't told me?*

Man: *Nah. It was okay.*

Woman: *Talk to me, honey. I can't believe you're not excited to be getting up and into things today. Are you sure you feel okay?*

Man: *I'm all right.*

This is obviously a substandard encounter, one that will go nowhere fast. It is likely to end either in a day of cold silence or loud conflict. The woman has tried hard to reach out to her husband, to establish a point of intimacy where hearts can touch, but he is proving to be untouchable. She is trying to get a preoccupied man to respond, but it isn't working. Maybe she'll be more successful later in the day, but maybe she'll give up trying before then.

Take a look at the man's responses. He deflects her questions and comments with level-one clichés as a goaltender deflects pucks in a hockey game. If he persists, he will slowly shut off her desire to enter his life and establish intimacy. Their relationship will suffer that day because of it, and the relationship will suffer even more significantly if he chooses to treat her the same way day after day.

Level Two

John Powell likes to talk about a second level of communication, a level he calls facts and reports.

At this level there is much conversation, but it is all based on an exchange of information about things beyond or external to the lives of the two people involved. The communication may center on things of mutual or momentary significance, but it lacks personal response or involvement. This is not the talk of two people who share intimacy about life. Without much effort, a level-two conversation could happen between two colleagues in a company dining room.

We've learned from talking with many married couples that, all too often, husbands and wives remain on level two for days, months, or years. As a result, the relationship doesn't grow, intimacy isn't developed, and two people don't progress much further beyond being housemates.

Let's return to the simulated dialogue. When we use it with groups of people, we tell them to imagine that the earlier conversation continues. It has now progressed to the second level. We challenge them to see how factual it appears to be but how lacking in any sense of intimacy or connection of hearts.

Man: *I noticed a pile of mail on the hallway table. Anything significant?*

Woman: *Lots of second-class stuff, a letter from your mother, the tuition bill from the college, . . . oh, and an invitation to a banquet. You'll also find an article there that I cut from the newspaper.*

Man: *An article? What is it about?*

Woman: *Sort of a dumb story on the front page the other night. Some wealthy guy that decided to set the Guinness world record for eating the world's most expensive meal.*

Man: *Why would you want me to read an article like that?*

Woman: *Just want you to read it. We'll talk about it later. Now what's on your list to do today?*

Man: *I'm headed for the electronics store as soon as it opens at ten.*

Woman: *How come?*

Man: *Didn't you look at the big ad in the paper that I told you about before I left for California? They've got stereos on sale. The best ones they sell—digital readouts, lots of buttons.*

Woman: *Buttons?*

Man: *Umm. You know. The new stereos have buttons and slides and switches all over the place. You can do anything with them.*

Woman: *Why buy a new stereo when the one we've got works just fine?*

Man: *Hey, a family's got to have a new stereo every few years, don't you think? Besides, the kids seem to have taken over the one we have, and I think it's probably beginning to wear out, and. . . .*

Woman: *And?*

Man: *Well, those buttons are like nothing I've ever seen before.*

Woman: *Before you go, please read the article on the table in the hallway.*

Man: *Yeah.*

Again, this is a routine conversation. It could happen in any home or apartment, in any relationship. There is little to attract one's attention or curiosity. We have learned a few facts, but what do we know about them? Very little.

There is nothing wrong with conversation on level two; a high percentage of our conversation is on this level. What would be sad is if this was as far as talk between the two went. We're going to demonstrate in the next chapter that the woman in this conversation had some strong concerns about what her husband was going to do that day, but in this conversation, she doesn't choose to share them or even suggest that she has them.

Gail: *If her husband can't accept her concerns and encourage her to bring them to the surface, why should she express them? Perhaps she's learned that it's safer to stay at level two.*

Gordon: *If she stays there, and he creates the conditions that keep the two of them there, this relationship is a loser. It's better than staying on level one, but not much better.*

Gail: *There's no hope on level one. Gordon, if you had responded like the man you played in the level-one dialogue, our marriage would never have stayed healthy. You know, when I play the woman's role in that scene, I always have the sickish feeling that comes from trying to care and being told that your caring doesn't count.*

Gordon: *All his clichés are obviously a cover-up. He wants to get away from the world, from his work, from her, maybe even from himself. Do you think she should have waited for a better time?*

Gail: *Maybe. I know I sometimes have to wait for a better time with you. When you are in an inward frame of mind, the harder I push you in conversation, the deeper inside yourself you will* *retreat. I sometimes feel as if I'm looking for you in a dark cave, so I work hard at being sensitive to this.*

Gordon: *You do a good job of giving me space and privacy when I need it.*

Gail: *Now let's go beyond levels one and two and get to more rewarding levels of communication.*

9

Going to the Bottom

Gail: *I just finished reading a story about Thomas Carlyle. The writer says that Carlyle was perceived as a tough, blunt, unfeeling man, but underneath that facade was a man who saw himself as affectionate and loving.*

Gordon: *That's a hard man to know.*

Gail: *Exactly. He dearly loved his wife, but was never able to express that love to her convincingly. He simply traveled through his marriage assuming she knew what was going on in his heart.*

Gordon: *You mean he never communicated his feelings to her? No words? No gestures?*

Gail: *Apparently not. He never said anything and never really did anything that would have revealed what he felt for her.*

Gordon: *You're describing a pretty difficult marriage.*

Gail: *The writer says that when Carlyle's wife died, he became distraught. He became obsessed with trying to find out whether or not she knew how much he'd loved her.*

Gordon: *What did he do?*

Gail: *He found her diaries and started reading them, hoping he'd find comments about their relationship. He was horrified when he discovered that she hadn't the slightest sense of his feelings for her. She died believing she was totally unloved.*

Gordon: *He found nothing that reflected on the marriage?*

Gail: *Nothing positive. In fact, the only comments he did find about their relationship centered on her resentment of his temper. Apparently he had a hot one, and she'd felt it more than once.*

Gordon: *What an awful discovery!*

Gail: *It almost killed him. He wished that she could return for just five minutes so he could pour out his love for her.*

Gordon: *I wonder how often that kind of remorse haunts people today?*

Gail: *More than we could possibly imagine, I suspect.*

Level Three

We come now to the third of John Powell's five levels of conversation, and this one is significantly deeper than the two we've already described. He called it the level of opinions and judgments. What makes this one more profound than the others is that when people talk to each other at this level, they share something of their deeper selves.

When we speak our opinions, we attach something of our inner mind or heart to our words. We become a bit more vulnerable as we throw out our own conclusions and reactions to situations and circumstances, and an element of risk begins to enter the picture.

At level three, sentences often begin with phrases such as, "I think" or "It seems to me" or "If you want my opinion" or "The way I see it. . . ." With those sentences comes the possibility that we could be wounded, demeaned, or squelched by anyone who wants to take advantage of our vulnerability.

In level-three conversation, the expression of opinion and judgment opens the door to our deeper thoughts, our convictions, and our insights. These come from our hidden world, and we expose them more freely to those we trust. We expose them more guardedly in situations where we are not sure whom we can trust. There we anticipate the possibility of being rebutted, of being told that we're foolish, or even of being laughed at.

In the continuing dialogue that we've written to illustrate these levels of conversation, we went deeper in the saga of a husband and wife on a Saturday morning who are dealing with an issue about which they both have opinions. Their personal agendas are only beginning to surface when the husband returns from a shopping trip and says,

Man: *I'm back from the electronics store.*

Woman: *What happened there?*

Man: *You wouldn't believe all the stuff they've got on sale. They have a new speaker so powerful that it could break the front picture window.*

Woman: *I've been praying for years for a speaker that could break our picture window.*

Man: *They've got an amplifier on sale that is three times more powerful than the one we've got. I was thrilled at what that set could do. And the buttons. . . .*

Woman: *Did you buy it?*

Man: *Well, no. I thought I ought to get you to go back with me and pick out which one you wanted: the oak cabinets or the maple ones.*

Woman: *Did you ever ask yourself whether I might have an opinion on the speakers themselves?*

Man: *You have an opinion on speakers?*

Woman: *Did you think to ask me whether I had an opinion about the kind of wattage the amplifier ought to have?*

Man: *You have an opinion about amplifier wattage?*

Woman: *Did it ever occur to you to ask me whether I thought we should buy a new stereo?*

Man: *You have an opinion about the stereo?*

Woman: *Yes, I do have an opinion—a strong one. And you've never asked about it.*

Man: *I didn't think you had an opinion. I didn't think you cared.*

Woman: *I care a lot about this decision to buy a new expensive stereo, and I've watched you avoid asking me what I thought ever since you started making noises about your intentions.*

Man: *I figured you'd tell me if you had a problem, and you must have one. What do you want to tell me?*

Woman: *I don't think I want to talk about it until you've read the newspaper article on the front hall table. Then I'll be ready to discuss new stereos.*

The good news is that the woman's hidden world is beginning to reach the light of day. Anyone who has had similar exchanges knows that these two are at a critical junction in their conversation. The door to the woman's thoughts lies open, but with a few simple destructive remarks, the man can slam it shut. If he chooses to slam it shut and repeats that process in other conversations, he will hear fewer and fewer of her opinions and judgments in the future. On those occasions when he does hear them, it will be under great duress, with the likelihood of strong and painful conflict. He obviously must be very careful about what he says next.

If this man is smart and perceptive, he will have picked up several signals in his wife's last few remarks. She is hurt that she has not been consulted about a decision that affects her. She may be insulted because he thinks she is not smart enough to have an interest in the technical aspects of the decision. She is offended that he feels he can move through this process without stopping to ask if she has something to offer.

If the man wants the kind of intimacy with his wife where two hearts touch, he needs to be very careful at this point. She has clearly shown that she has opinions on the subject. The door is open, and he had better look inside gently and with reverence.

Looking back, we can now begin to see why the man had stayed on levels one or two regarding this decision. If he could stay rather light and uninvolved, he could do exactly what he wanted. He could arrive home with several boxes and simply announce the arrival of a new stereo. You can do that in a relationship that never goes beyond level one or two. Convenient? Yes, of course. But remember, it provides no intimacy.

A previous conversation at a lighter level might have gone like this:

Man: *I've been wondering if it isn't time for us to think about a new sound system. The old one is entirely worn-out, but you know how much I enjoy good music, and I'd really like to investigate the possibility of getting a new one.*

Woman: *I'm not sure I agree, but it doesn't hurt to do some looking and talking. Seems to me that we've been spending a lot of money lately.*

Man: *You're right about the spending, but this is the time of the year when things go on sale, and stereos will probably never get this cheap again. I'd like to go down on Saturday after I get back from California. Come with me?*

Woman: *If you'll buy me breakfast.*

Level Four

Levels of talking need to go even further. As we have studied Powell's perspective, we've taken certain liberties in order to suggest that one could call the fourth level that of feelings and intuitions.

This is a level at which many people rarely feel safe. Some people express their feelings and intuitions in a negative way: in anger, with tears, with the anticipation that they're going to be blasted by a "Carlyle type" who will take their heads off.

But when people express their feelings in a healthy way, they are beginning to open up the deepest parts of their lives. They are not necessarily speaking with the authority of logic and reason, but rather from areas of their inner lives that go beyond words. They are talking about how their emotions and their hearts respond to various situations.

When a person speaks at the fourth level of feelings and intuition, he is free to say, "I feel sad today" or "I'm just plain down." This is a level where one can say, "I don't know why, but I'm scared about where all this is leading." Another is speaking at this level when she can say to a friend, "The whole thing just makes me very angry and hurt." "I'm feeling dissatisfied about all of this," someone else says. "Down deep inside I don't feel right about this." "I could be wrong, of course, but my gut tells me. . . ."

Positive feelings also can and need to be expressed when people are conversing at level four:

"You know, I really like it when you're around."

"I feel good about this project."

"A day like this brings me more happiness than I could have ever imagined."

Many people are reluctant or unable to talk on level four. Temperamentally, they are wired to distrust feelings and intuitions—those of others or their own. They are attracted by only one thing: the truth as it is described in facts, statistics, and events. They are put off by those who start sentences with a declaration of feelings. They are so put off, sometimes, that they avoid such people or—when avoidance is impossible—ridicule or belittle them. This is probably what happened all too often in the Carlyle marriage.

Feelings and intuitions are neither good nor evil—they just are. Of course they can sometimes be inaccurate or blown out of proportion, and if they become a person's exclusive guiding star for all choices and conclusions, there may well be serious fallout in life. What we're saying is that extreme avoidance of feelings or extreme dependence upon them are equally unacceptable.

Many people have concluded that they are safest when they keep their feelings to themselves. As children, their feelings may have been ignored, repudiated, even punished. As teenagers, their feelings may have been laughed at or gossiped about. Few things register more profoundly in the heart than mistreatment of our feelings. Deep hurt or humiliation can cause people to suppress them so that they not only never express them to others but even avoid acknowledging them to themselves.

A close friend tells of a day in his childhood when his father in a moment of rage threw a light bulb at him. It missed the side of his head by inches and exploded when it hit the wall behind him. He was terrified, but when he expressed his feeling to his mother, she told him that his father was "just kidding around." In her attempt to make everything okay, she inadvertently did damage to her son. In effect she told him that his feeling wasn't accurate, when in fact it was. It was normal to be terrified. In putting an untruthful interpretation on the event and therefore implying that his feeling was wrong, she contributed to a process that made it difficult for him to trust his feelings or feel good about expressing them later in his adult life.

Some of us have had the experience of having our disclosed feelings used against us at a later date. What has been told in confidence is brought to light in the future, when a former friend emerges as an enemy. This only needs to happen a few times before one becomes reluctant to deal at the feelings level again.

Let's return to the dialogue again. Now the level-four dimension has been added to the conversation. This is a crucial time. The man or the woman can take advantage of the expressed vulnerability and hurt the other or bring light to the situation that will make whatever happens a good decision for everyone.

Man: *I read the article on the hall table.*

Woman: *Oh. What did you think?*

Man: *Well, at first I was amused at the stupidity of it all, then I found myself getting a little bit angry.*

Woman: *Angry? About what?*

Man: *There are millions of people living in poverty in this world—Africa, Asia, even the streets of American cities. They haven't had a decent meal in who knows how long? Then this guy spends $104,000 on a meal, simply to set a world record. Why does the press cover such stupid things, anyway? The more I read, the madder I got.*

Woman: *Mad? Tell me exactly what made you so mad.*

Man: *Well, he had enough food to eat at normal prices. What business did he have going out and spending all that when he didn't need to?*

Woman: *If there are lots of people in the world starving, a person really doesn't have the right to spend exorbitant sums of money on his own personal enjoyment? That's a strong statement.*

Man: *Sometimes we have to make strong statements so we can see ourselves as others see us. There's too much materialism and hedonism going on in this world, and it's getting out of con-*

trol. People buying things just because there's something new to buy. If it isn't more elegant dining, it's a third or fourth car, and then it's houses, and then it's boats, and then it's. . . .

Woman: *Stereo sets.*

Man: *Stereo sets? (pause) Yes, but. . . .*

Woman: *I was thinking the same thing you're thinking. (another pause) It really got to bothering me.*

Man: *Bothering you?*

Woman: *Bothering is a good word for it. I had the same feelings going through me when you headed for the electronics store that I knew you would have when you read about the rich man and his expensive meal.*

Man: *Feelings? What kind?*

Woman: *A bit of sadness at first. Then some anger. But most of all a feeling of disturbance that we're not in control of our buying habits.*

Man: *Maybe I ought to read through the article again.*

Intimacy is growing here. Two people have found a way to send and receive conversational signals at a deep level. Two people are expressing what they feel inside and are beginning to hear what the other is saying.

When we hear someone express himself at this level, our response should not be "That's a bad feeling" or "That's a good feeling." The question ought to be, How can I best offer companionship to the one who has expressed him or herself in such a way? Does this person need encouragement to say more? Does he or she need to be left alone for a while? Should I laugh with them or cry with them? Is there a need for simple, open listening? Or, in the case of the husband and wife in this dialogue, is the conversation heading toward a point where someone is going to have to say, "I need to do some more thinking"?

At level four, there is little need for answers; there is simply a need to be heard.

Level Five

The deepest of the conversational levels we have come to call that of maximum truth. This is a level where one is most likely to find joy—all the positive qualities that our inner being imagines possible in a relationship of real intimacy. This is the level where two hearts touch. Of course, there is also likely to be pain at this level, because truth can be painful, but it is a "clean" pain, the kind that heals and builds.

When we communicate with spouses, friends, or children on level five, we are dealing with exchanges such as affirmation or rebuke, confession or forgiveness. Here dreams and disillusionments are revealed. This is where the great defining moments of a relationship occur, where we make a profound, life-changing choice together and arrive at a mutual insight that eventuates in growth.

Let's return one more time to our fictional couple. We've watched them go from clichés to some rather frank discussion about values. The conversation is reaching a defining moment, one that determines whether or not disagreement can be turned into a positive experience. Watch how the two of them seek to find common ground, how they try to avoid unnecessary criticism, and how they try to leave each other's dignity intact.

Man: *Did you actually have the stereo store in mind when you put that article out there for me to read?*

Woman: *Yeah, I did. I've lived with you long enough to know that it would trigger your sensitivities.*

Man: *But that means you knew I had a new stereo in mind even before I told you.*

Woman: *I've lived with you long enough to know how you prepare me for these decisions. You left the newspaper ad out in the middle of the room when you left for California. Instead of saying what you wanted to do, you hoped the message would sink in when the ad caught my eye.*

Man: *And so when you saw the article you. . . .*

Woman: *When I saw it, I suspected it might say more to you than I could. You left an ad for me; I clipped an article for you.*

Man: *What you're really telling me is that you don't think I should go down there this afternoon and buy all those buttons.*

Woman: *If it's buttons you want, I've got a drawer full of them in the basement. But if it's integrity you want, I'd like to see you do some more thinking. I think you'll be sorry you spent all that money 48 hours after the money-back guarantee runs out.*

Man: *What makes you so sure of that?*

Woman: *Because I've spent more than a few years figuring you out. I know that down in your heart you really don't believe we should spend all the money we're capable of making. I know you well enough to be sure that you sometimes make a buying decision that you come to regret soon after. And I know that you're tough and humble enough to face the truth when someone gives you another version of it.*

Man: *Why do you know all that?*

Woman: *Because twenty-five years of living with you convinced me that you have a heart to do things God's way.*

Man: *So what you're saying is that you think I'm in danger of making a bad decision today, and you want me to think about it more.*

Woman: *You couldn't have heard me more clearly.*

Man: *I guess I'm disappointed, because I was lying in bed this morning, imagining that sound system in our living room.*

All of that enthusiasm blotted out what you knew all the time: There is an even deeper conviction that we've got to be more restrained. Thanks for helping me to see that. But. . . .

Woman: *But?*

Man: *But the maple speaker cabinets would have looked nice in the living room.*

Woman: *How about brunch? It won't set a Guinness record, but it will do.*

There is affirmation in level-five conversation whenever a person shares the potentials and possibilities he has seen in the other. In a sense, when we affirm others, we believe in their present value and their future potential. We have seen their lives, and we want them to know that we place value on them. We all desperately need this form of level-five conversation.

Goethe wrote: "When we treat a man as he is, we make him worse than he is. When we treat him as if he already were what he potentially could be, we make him what he should be."

At critical times during His earthly mission, Jesus Christ was affirmed by His Heavenly Father. Coming out of the water of the Jordan River where He had been baptized, Christ heard the voice of His Father: "This is my Son, whom I love; with him I am well pleased" (Matthew 3:17 NIV). The Father gave His Son both a sense of belonging and value, even before His active ministry began. On the Mount where He was transfigured, Jesus was again affirmed by the Father in front of others. This time it's a word about competence: "Listen to him."

No doubt these reminders of His Father's love carried Jesus through many difficult moments. Perhaps the chief agony on the cross was that Jesus perceived a strange and unprecedented absence of the Father as He bore the sins of human-kind. You could say that His great pain was the momentary loss of experiencing His Father's affirmation.

A lovely young child, Molly Sell, worships with her family in our New York City congregation. One day she was with her mother, Peggy, who was driving to an appointment some-where in Manhattan. "We need to ask Jesus to help us find a parking place," Peggy said to her daughter.

Molly agreed and immediately began to pray. "Dear Jesus, please help us to find a parking place and help Daddy at work and help Patrick and Olin at school, and Ingrid, too. Amen."

"Did you like my prayer, Mommy?" Molly quickly asked. "Did you notice that I didn't pray for myself? Isn't it won-derful that I'm such a humble person?"

This is a request for Peggy to stamp value on both the content and the spirit of Molly's prayer—and on Molly her-self. It's an instant level-five moment, and it's affirmational in character.

William Barclay recounts how the great painter Benjamin West got his start. Affirmation was the key.

> One day [West's] mother went out leaving him in charge of his little sister, Sally. In his mother's absence he discovered some bottles of colored ink and began to paint Sally's portrait. In doing so he made a considerable mess of things with ink blots all over. His mother came back. She saw the mess but said nothing. She picked up the piece of paper and saw the drawing. "Why," she said, "it's Sally!" and stooped and kissed him. Ever after Benjamin West used to say, "My mother's kiss made me a painter." (*Ephesians: The Daily Study Bible*, West-minster, 1976.)

Our words of affirmation can be the "kiss" that motivates growth and development, self-worth, and desire. We grow best in an environment in which those who believe in us are unashamed to communicate that belief.

Level-fives happen all the time when people are pursuing intimacy. A father communicates affirming words to a daughter who struggles with puberty. A friend affirms another as she struggles with the demands of a new job. A wife affirms a husband who is learning how to take care of tasks about the home that he used to think were "women's work." Affirmation is one of the deepest communicative conversations. All of us need it.

Rebuke

Rebuke is sometimes needed, too, at level five. In the biblical sense, rebuke is confronting a person with the consequences of poor choices. The rebuke compares a person's actions with the laws of God when he has become temporarily blind to what is happening.

In the Old Testament, King Ahab of Israel saw a piece of property he very badly wanted to own. He made the property owner, Naboth, an offer, and it was refused. Ahab returned to his palace and became sullen. He literally went to his bed, turned his face to the wall, and wept.

This was the perfect time for a rebuke. Someone could have been of great help by pointing out to Ahab the absurdity of his childish reactions.

But Queen Jezebel apparently knew nothing about level five. Instead of rebuking her husband, she attached herself to his feelings and set into motion events that cost Naboth his life and brought the coveted property into Ahab's hands. In this case, the lack of a rebuke ruined the lives of two men.

In the New Testament we see a positive biblical example. The Apostle Paul loved the congregation at Corinth, although it is sometimes difficult to understand why, and he loved them enough to rebuke them with force.

"I wrote you out of great distress and anguish of heart and with many tears, not to grieve you but to let you know the depth of my love for you" (2 Corinthians 2:4 NIV). Paul loved the Corinthians too much to allow his intimacy with them to collapse for want of communication on the fifth level. This is no light moment for him. In fact, this is the only valid basis for biblical rebuke—it should sober us and bring sadness to have to hurt another. If we study Paul's rebukes, it becomes clear that he gave them because he valued the long-term relationship he built with people. He would risk the pain of a negative reaction because he knew it would be profitable in the end.

A loving rebuke on level five is part of any intimate relationship. Its intensity depends upon how great the intimacy is or how deep the people involved want intimacy to be. Rebukes are exchanged between those who have proved their care and concern for each other: between mentors and followers, where there has been a history of credibility and faithfulness; between a parent and a child; between spouses. A rebuke is not merely an angry expostulation. It is an expression of loving concern that one earns the right to offer.

Among many Christians there can be plenty of criticism and gossip, but there are relatively few who are skillful at rebuke. Often we allow good friends and associates to move toward some form of personal destruction because we are afraid to confront them with the truth. Not to rebuke when a rebuke would be timely is unfortunate.

Of course some will not accept a rebuke. We have all seen the person who bristles with anger at the slightest indication of disagreement or confrontation. Such a person has decided that always being right or being beyond helpful criticism is more important than intimacy.

In the days of John Adams and Thomas Jefferson, there was a period when their friendship fell into grave, seemingly unresolvable conflict. It was Dr. Benjamin Rush, a fellow signer of the Declaration of Independence, who wrote to Adams, imploring him to heal the breech between himself and Jefferson.

Call it a loving rebuke. Rush faced Adams with the open sore of the conflict. At first, Adams put up strong protests of innocence.

> Why do you make so much of nothing? Of what use can it be for Jefferson and me to exchange letters? I have nothing to say to him, but to wish him an easy journey to heaven, when he goes, which I wish may be delayed, as long as life shall be agreeable to him. And he can have nothing to say to me, but to bid me make haste and be ready. Time and chance, however, or possibly design, may produce ere long a letter between us. (*Abigail Adams* by Dorothie Bobbe, Putnam, 1966.)

But Adams was more willing to accept rebuke than he first appeared. Although he seemed to strongly resist Benjamin Rush's expression of concern, he nevertheless wrote to Jefferson six days later, and their friendship—dormant for almost eight years—was restored.

On the fifth level, people find the ability not only to affirm and rebuke, but also to confess and forgive. One feels the freedom to say a genuine "I'm sorry. I blew it!" Another feels free to say, "I forgive you." Those are hard words for some, and more than one intimate connection has cooled because one of the persons involved, having offended the other, was unable to face up to his insensitivity or offense and acknowledge it with a confession of wrongdoing.

"He just finds it impossible to say I'm sorry," someone says about another. But the inability to deal with confession means that relationships of all sorts will be restricted. Confession and forgiveness mean that short accounts are being kept in a relationship. Proud people allow accounts to go on longer and longer and walls to grow thicker and thicker. Finally the relationship can no longer take the weight of so many unresolved hurts, and it breaks down.

Our dear friend, the late Dr. Paul Rees, in writing a brief biography of John William Fletcher, a great Methodist preacher in the days of John Wesley, tells of a day when another clergyman, Thomas Reader, read one of Fletcher's books and became so incensed that he immediately began a three-day journey to the author's home to tell him off.

> On arrival at the vicarage, [Reader] knocked loudly on the door. To the servant who answered the knock he presented his request for an interview with the vicar. No sooner had the servant announced the gentleman's name than Fletcher, recognizing it, hastened from his study to receive the visitor, and spreading out his hands, he exclaimed, "Come in, come in, thou blessed of the Lord! Am I so honored as to receive a visit from so esteemed a servant of my master? Let's have a little prayer while refreshments are getting ready."
>
> Mr. Reader was so puzzled, taken aback, overcome. Although he spent three days in the vicarage, he was unable to muster enough courage to even broach the subject that had been seething in his heart. He later testified that "he never enjoyed three days of such spiritual and profitable intercourse in all his life." (Speech given by Paul Rees at John Fletcher College.)

What a remarkable forgiving spirit Fletcher revealed! Because he was such a man, the relationship between himself and one who could have become a bitter enemy became intense friendship and growth. That's a form of intimacy.

At this fifth level of communication, one is also free to speak of dreams and disillusionments. It is a special relationship, indeed, when we are able to open our deepest desires and struggles to another and know that our words will be carefully weighed and appreciated.

When communication is established at level five, it provides a base for strength when crisis comes. What some do not understand is that if the base has not been established before there is stress or pressure, the relationship will most likely break down when crisis comes.

Philip Yancey writes of John and Claudia Claxton, who found themselves battling with her Hodgkin's disease and the possibility that death was imminent. When Yancey visited with them and tried to analyze what was at the root of the strength of their relationship, John Claxton, a chaplain's assistant in a hospital, told him this:

> I have seen dying patients in hospitals. It's not like on the TV shows or in the movies like AIRPORT. In the movies, couples who have fought for years, in the face of danger, suddenly forget their differences and come together. Life doesn't work that way, however.
>
> When a couple meets a crisis, the result is a caricature of what's already there in their relationship. We happened to deeply love each other and had open communication. Therefore the crisis drove us to each other. We were unified and we trusted each other. Feelings of blame and anger against each other did not creep in. The crisis of Claudia's illness merely brought to the surface and magnified feelings already present. (*Where Is God When It Hurts?* Zondervan, 1977.)

That strong witness to a relationship under fire through illness is what communication is all about. Simply put, those who have dug deeply to level five know how to talk and be heard. Only in this way will intimacy grow and enlarge so that two hearts can touch.

We understand this by experience. We know what it is like to walk together through very dark days when—so it seemed—all we had was each other and our ability to commune with each other and God. On level five we knew how to acknowledge the great sorrow of failure and how to say yes to the granting of mercy. Neither of us is sure that we would have survived the darkest days if level five had been strange territory to us.

We return to the earlier story of Mahler, the great composer. There he sits, with the power to communicate with a young man and give him hope in response to his effort. He cannot do it, brilliant musician though he is. He cannot communicate on level one, even, nor level two, three, or four, much less five.

Then there is John William Fletcher, who knew how to turn an enemy into a friend. It took seconds for him to bring a would-be critic to levels four and five and create a friendship rich in spiritual intimacy.

The difference between Mahler and Fletcher? Communication.

Gail: *Sometimes people feel that good communication happens when two people are very similar, but I think our personalities are quite different.*

Gordon: *You are more of a realist; I'm more of an idealist.*

Gail: *Well, you're always able to see the possible, the big picture, the new and ever-changing. I am more concerned about structures, routines, details, and practicalities. When we were first married, I always wanted to bring you back to solid ground every time you started dreaming.*

Gordon: *But you quickly learned to give me freedom to paint my dreams out loud.*

Gail: *That's because I quickly realized that we practical people can easily stifle the dreams and possibility thinking of our loved ones.*

Gordon: *If we couldn't share our dreams with each other, we would have to abandon level-five communication and diminish the intimacy of our relationship.*

10

When Things Grow Sullen

Gordon: *Have you ever thought about how much conflict there is in our marriage?*

Gail: *We've had a few difficult moments, but you make it sound as if we disagree all the time.*

Gordon: *There's a sense in which we do.*

Gail: *When was the last time we had a conflict?*

Gordon: *We're having one right now.*

Gail: *This isn't a conflict. It's a discussion.*

Gordon: *But we're not seeing something the same way, are we? We're in disagreement over words and a rather important concept.*

Gail: *But this isn't conflict. Conflict is where you really get hot and blow off some steam.*

Gordon: *That's what I'd call destructive conflict. You and I don't have much of that.*

Gail: *What are you talking about, then?*

Gordon: *I'm saying that we conflict regularly. We share our perspectives and conclusions about a lot of things, even when they aren't the same. You can tell me that you don't agree, and I can usually do the same with you.*

Gail: *That's conflict?*

Gordon: *Any time two minds diverge, you have conflict. You and I don't mind thinking out loud and sharing our points of*

139

view. We enjoy hearing each other's perspective, even when it isn't in synch with our own. Neither of us feels under pressure to surrender when we see things differently. That's constructive conflict.

Gail: *So conflict happens all the time. It only becomes destructive when you decide you have to win or make the other person lose or you feel you have to humiliate the other person.*

Gordon: *The best discussions between two people are often conflict-oriented. They're the kind that cause growth. They sharpen the mind. Out of them come new insights and understandings.*

Gail: *It would be a dull life if that sort of thing didn't happen, wouldn't it?*

Gordon: *Sure. So you see why I'm delighted that we have the ability to conflict.*

Gail: *I wish you'd find a better word for it.*

Gordon: *How about skirmish?*

Gail: *I'm more comfortable with conflict. But don't tell anyone we do this; they'll never understand.*

We like the story of a man who was being pursued by a roaring, hungry lion. Feeling the animal's hot breath upon the back of his neck and concluding that his time had come, he cried out in desperation, "O Lord, please make this lion a Christian."

The supplication seemed effective, because within seconds the fleeing man saw the lion stop and assume a kneeling position. Then he saw the lion fold its paws and begin to move its lips, as if in prayer. Greatly relieved at this remarkable turn of events and desirous of showing a forgiving spirit, the man decided to join the now-docile lion in his meditation. But as he came near, he heard the lion say, "Bless, O Lord, this food for which I am exceedingly grateful."

This is a story about assumptions—bad ones—the kind that bite you.

How about the bad assumption that Christian relationships are devoid of conflict and that if people are followers of Christ, all will be peace and tranquility?

There may be bad assumptions involved when Christian businessmen form a partnership. There's nothing wrong with two Christians developing a business arrangement. The problems arise if they think that nothing can go wrong *because* they are Christians.

"I know it is going to be tremendous for us," one partner says. "This relationship won't have any of the problems I normally have. We even pray together before we begin our meetings. How can you get into trouble when that sort of thing is happening?"

Our fears about this assumption were realized when the two partners found themselves on the verge of litigation two years later. Being Christians did not guarantee that they could resolve disagreements about policies and practices, even with prayer before each meeting. Their first difficulty was in assuming that Christians never conflict. Their second was in assuming that confessing Christ means the other will never be disagreeable. As we said before: bad assumptions.

It seems strange but necessary to say that no relationship will last long without conflict, including those involving Christians. Conflict is an inevitable part of communication. To the extent that we are thinking people with values, convictions, perspectives, and feelings, all of us are going to find ourselves in disagreement with others on various occasions. Conflict is not necessarily wrong or bad; it can be a path to personal and relational growth. Conflict managed correctly can lead to intimacy.

A classic example of conflict can be found in the relationship of two writers: H. L. Mencken and Theodore Dreiser. Richard Lingerman, Dreiser's biographer, says that Dreiser once inscribed a book. "To H. L. Mencken, my oldest living enemy." Lingerman goes on to say, "Those exasperated words summed up one of the most seminal and longest friendships in American letters."

The two writers had a stormy friendship. Mencken often reviewed Dreiser's books with vitriolic criticism. Lingerman adds:

> Religious, political and temperamental differences accounted for the rest. Those differences were so marked that it is surprising that they remained friends for nearly 40 years—minus the time when they weren't speaking to each other.
>
> Neither man had exposed his inner feelings to the other. Dreiser was more emotional than Mencken; but he was also more prone to explosions of temper and punitive silences. But now, at least, they were more willing to agree to disagree, and they tried harder to avoid misunderstandings. (*New York Times* Book Review, March 8, 1992.)

Their relationship fell on very hard times when Theodore Dreiser made a brief visit to Mencken's Baltimore home. Dreiser was ill when he arrived, and Mencken was suffering because his aged mother died while Dreiser was still visiting him.

When news of Mencken's mother's death came to the house, Dreiser appeared to offer no consolation, remaining silent. It was as if he didn't care, and Mencken was horrified. This seeming offense divided the two, and Mencken followed it by writing harsh reviews of Dreiser's later novels.

Only years later did Mencken learn that he had completely misinterpreted Dreiser's actions during that day of intense grief. He had failed to hear Dreiser's attempts at offering sympathy, and he had not realized that Dreiser's personality was such that he could only acknowledge sorrow for his friend by being silent. Two friends had missed each other's signals; conflict was the result; and an intimate, lifelong friendship was destroyed.

When Dreiser died in 1945, a friend telegraphed Mencken the news and concluded, "He loved you." Mencken could only reply, "Theodore's death leaves me feeling as if my whole world had blown up. . . . He was my captain in a war that will never end, and we had a swell time together. No other man had a greater influence upon my youth."

Biblical Conflicts

A modern story such as this can be matched by biblical ones. How biblical people resolved some of their conflicts provides an interesting primer on the subject of reconciliation.

Can you imagine, for example, the disciples clashing with Jesus? Remember the day Simon Peter disagreed with Jesus over the course of the future and the Lord's announcement that He would die at the hands of his enemies? Peter utterly rejected Jesus' perspective of the cross. Jesus' reaction was a loving but tough one. He said something like "Get behind me, Satan." These are not words calculated to pour oil on troubled waters.

Conflict was present the day the impatient disciples attempted to bar small children from being brought to Jesus for blessing. One suspects the disciples were clearly embarrassed when Jesus reversed their decision.

Do you recall the dramatic storm scene on Lake Galilee? What else can it be called but angry discord when the disciples surrounded the sleeping figure of Christ, accusing Him of not caring for their terrifying situation? "Don't you care if we die?" they screamed. Later there would be friction over what should be done to take care of 5,000 people who had pursued Jesus into the wilderness. Jesus said they should be fed; the disciples thought they should be sent away.

There was conflict when the disciples argued among themselves over who was the greatest; there was more conflict when they argued over the reports that Christ had risen from the dead.

We tend to imagine that good people with noble intentions do not conflict, but history actually proves the opposite. When we study the relationships of Christians in the Book of Acts, there emerges a startling amount of material on the subject of disagreement. In fact antagonism seemed to be part of the normal life-style of the early Christians. Say all you want about their love for one another, but don't try to pretend that their love wasn't mixed with struggle.

We are convinced that in every human relationship is a spirit of dissimulation: a force or energy that works to divide people and cause them to defy one another. No relationship starts at square one; it begins at square minus three. No matter how much we say we care for one another, there are underlying energies which will try to polarize us—if not at first, then later, when our defenses are down, when we are a bit bored, when we are feeling stress.

Christians often bring to their relationships a highly defined agenda. A Christian marriage, for instance, involves two people who are earnest about bringing the best God has to offer into their home. They are not going to be without opinions about how that should be done.

Christian friends have a game plan that is more than just the pursuit of fun and amusement, and when people move beyond that level of activity, there may be a clash of opinions as to where energies and resources should be allocated.

Furthermore, the church tends to draw people who describe life in terms of principles and laws. These people want answers to the great moral and ethical dilemmas of our day. They want to face up to the problem of sin and evil and know what to do about it. This intensity is inevitably going to create an atmosphere ripe for conflict as they compare and contrast their insights with others. Issues of personal life are more likely to be discussed and faced than in secular organizations. In Christian relationships, actions and attitudes that non-Christians would either avoid or ignore are often confronted and discussed.

Conflict often arises among Christians because of the stress of constant change. Lives are changing, circumstances are changing, and assignments to Christian service are changing—and change is always a challenge to our relationships.

Perhaps the greatest reason for conflict still lies in the fact that we are sinners. We are prone to selfishness, greed, covetousness, and anger unless we keep a vigilant guard upon ourselves. Things like these, unwatched, become a breeding ground for destructive conflict. Early Christians faced the same basic issues we live with in our world. Nothing really seems to have changed.

Take, for example, the first argument that appears in the Book of Acts (chapter 1). Someone had to take the place of apostolic leadership vacated by Judas Iscariot. Who was it to be? There is no indication of anger, but two candidates were put up by people who had different views as to who the new man ought to be. So an election of sorts was held to determine the mind of the Holy Spirit. A man named Matthias carried the vote.

What is admirable about the problem and its solution is the fact that when the process was completed and Matthias chosen, there is no indication of any further debate over the matter. The issue was closed. Election was the solution to the conflict, and it was resolved peaceably, as far as we can tell. Everyone was satisfied, apparently even the man who was not selected.

The first major conflict in the early church appears in Acts 6. Christian Jews of Hellenist origin protested that the Christian Jews of the Judean area were discriminating against their widows and orphans. Although everyone was giving generously to the support of the disadvantaged in the congregation, the generosity of the people was apparently being poorly administered. We do not know if the accusation included charges of negligence or whether it was merely a protest over the ineptness of the organization's leaders.

The important thing is that the conflict was surfaced and then resolved in a way that was pleasing to all concerned. When it was over, its results brought further growth to the congregation. The account is a remarkable model of conflict at its best, and ought to be studied carefully when people ponder struggle in relationships.

Rather than become defensive at the criticism against their leadership, the apostles handled the animosity by first surfacing it, not permitting it to remain at the murmur stage, where it could have been destructive. They acknowledged that a genuine case could be made, and the hint appears that they realized they were the victims of a clash of priorities.

To their credit, the aggrieved do not appear to have pressed their accusations but rather participated in the resolution of the problem. All engaged in the selection of spiritual men who would take the administration of funds from the shoulders of the apostles, who, by the way, seemed delighted to escape this burden.

If there is a key to the solution of the problem, it is this: The Hellenist Jews, who had just cause, were originally in danger of poorly handling their case. They were murmuring. But the Judean Jews, who seem to have been the root of the wrong, pursued the right solution. The results? The church grew. Conflict properly handled often makes growth happen in marriages, friendships, and congregations.

Later there was conflict between Peter and the elders of the church (Acts 11), when word reached Jerusalem that Peter had not only successfully preached to Gentiles and brought them to faith, but had actually accepted hospitality in a Gentile home. This was an unheard-of thing for a Jew to do (Christian or non-Christian).

Again, the confrontation is worth close study. The men caught in dispute examined the facts with open minds and hearts. If there was any hostility in their encounter, it was because they all were facing new realities and insights that went against the grain of all their traditions. But the facts reigned supreme in their thinking, and when the evidence of God's hand had been clearly presented and evaluated, conciliation quickly followed.

Acts 15 gives us the record of another significant conflict in the Christian community, one that could have split the early church wide open. Bible students refer to this event as the Jerusalem Council, a time when early Christian leaders convened to wrestle with the question, "What must Gentiles do in order to become followers of Christ?" Some conservative Jewish Christians had rather stringent ideas about what should be required; others, like Paul, pressed for a broader perspective. This time the dispute was vigorous, and it seemed at first as if there could be no way to work it out.

The resolution was a compromise that everyone could live with while still remaining reasonably faithful to their convictions. If there is something to be learned about conflict in Acts 15, it is that well-meaning Christians with strong beliefs found that compromise was more important than endlessly dividing from one another and creating a debilitating weakness to their fellowship and witness.

The Lessons of Conflict

What can we learn from those biblical conflicts? Several lessons and principles.

1. *In the best of conflicts, each side genuinely respected the opinions and judgments of the other.* They stuck to the issue.

All of us have seen and been part of conflicts where parties disagreeing with one another drifted from the real issue to personal attack. At such times, one's reputation, motives, and esteem may be called into question. There can be name-calling and accusation, resulting in unrestrained anger. It is not unusual for people to forget what the original purpose of the conflict was because so many other matters have insinuated themselves into the confrontation.

But when well-meaning people choose to respect one another, they can vigorously exchange views with the objective of discovering the greatest amount of truth in the situation. They are careful to make sure that only the issue itself stands between them.

2. *The relationship was more important than winning.* Put another way, in a uniquely Christian relationship, there are no winners or losers; there are only "growers." From the conflicts in Acts, you get the clear impression that the believers were most anxious to resolve their problems so that everyone would profit from the solutions. No one had to humiliate or intimidate another.

That is a very important matter. In marriages and friendships, if someone always feels a need to be vindicated, always has to feel triumphant in order to maintain a sense of self-esteem, the relationship will soon be destroyed. Some people do not feel free to admit to wrong at any point during a conflict. They may assume it would be too damaging to their sense of personhood. Thus they tend to enter into conflict with a do-or-die fervor. They are liable to find themselves much more anxious to win than to get at the truth, and that is destructive.

3. *There was a willingness to compromise when necessary.* This principle could make you feel uncomfortable, especially if you think of compromise as the way of the faithless or the spineless.

But remember the Jerusalem Council, which had compromise written all over it. We can learn something important from it. In many disputes, an obvious answer to the problem will not be forthcoming—at least not one that pleases all parties who are honestly expressing themselves. A compromise on the issue therefore becomes important. Compromise gives time for all involved to test the issue further and search for deeper insights and truths.

In a healthy environment of intimacy, this sort of compromise is going on all the time and is so common that people don't even know they're doing it. Imagine a mother and father arguing over how to handle a disobedient child. The father wants to know exactly what the child did, and he's prepared to punish on the basis of the information. But the mother is concerned about what led up to the child's choosing to be disobedient. She wants to take the measure of the child's present attitude about what happened. These are two reasonable approaches to the same problem, and a couple of well-meaning parents could get into trouble with each other if they aren't aware that their temperaments and perspectives lead them to ask questions differently.

4. *Unresolved conflicts left untended will fall into the wrong hands.*

If two people in conflict cannot bring their problem to a resolution within a reasonable amount of time, others will become involved.

That seems to have been Paul's great concern when he wrote to the Philippians and urged Euodia and Syntyche—two fine Christian women who had been leaders—to resolve their problems quickly. He was obviously concerned that their friction would escalate into a public conflict that might get out of control. He clearly feared that others might enter the fray on one side or another and rip the church apart. Help these women, Paul wrote. Get them together. Press them toward a healing and restoration of their former intimacy.

That sort of thing happens frequently in relationships. Children quickly begin to pick up the vibrations when their parents cannot resolve a conflict. A congregation suffers when some of its leaders begin to resist one another. Younger or less-mature Christians begin to debate the issues, start to take sides, and often permit the debate to get out of hand. That has been the most frequent source of church divisions.

5. *Anger has no place in conflict, except to provide energy for finding the truth.* A man or woman who has a temper will often "win" conflicts because almost everyone else is terrified of seeing the temper ignited, but intimacy will never grow in such an environment. Angry people like this make it nearly impossible to build a deep relationship. Out of self-preservation, one becomes more interested in keeping the lid on than in expressing a perspective and position. Men and women who cannot control their anger rarely find out what others are thinking; no one has the courage to risk an outburst by telling the truth.

When a person knows that he has a temper, he must be very careful to make sure he has it under control. He must not be permitted to destroy other people through intimidation.

6. *There is a kernel of truth in virtually every point made in a conflict.* We must learn to look and listen for it. In conflict, people often express feelings, opinions, and judgments that they would otherwise never have made known. Much of this is good, and others have to learn to watch for such expressions. When truth surfaces in conflict, it can become very valuable, if we know how to handle it.

Suppose a woman becomes jealous of a platonic friendship her boyfriend has with another woman. It eats at her and begins to change the way she responds to him, but she's afraid to express her feelings to him.

It's only when she raises the subject without recrimination or accusation that headway can be made. She starts by defining her perception. This is what she is seeing, and this is how she feels as a result. Both seek the kernel of truth in the matter.

He begins to see that what he thinks is innocent can be difficult for her to handle. She begins to see he is hearing an I-don't-trust-you message. Each has something valid to say to the other, and if one or both refuse to listen, the problem is on its way to destructiveness. But because they seek out the truthful center of each message, they find a resolution. He works to make her feel secure in his love; she works to increase and express her trust.

7. *Confession and forgiveness are an indispensable part of the resolution of conflict.*

One of the reasons Jesus said we have to become like children is that children do not normally hold grudges. Unfortunately, it is not too long before they learn from adults to hide or forget their own failures and expose or remember the failures of others.

To admit wrong and to ask forgiveness has been a family value we have pursued since the earliest days. To harbor resentments or grudges is even unhealthy for us physically.

Dr. E. Stanley Jones had a theory that our bodies are made for love, affirmation, forgiveness, cooperation, and kindness. Those responses are like oil to our physical machinery. When the opposite behaviors are chosen or permitted to prevail, it is like adding sand rather than oil to our machinery. Little wonder that we eventually grind to a halt under such circumstances. Little wonder that we end up in a hospital or in a therapist's office. The often-quoted statement "confession is good for the soul" is wiser than many people think.

We have had countless conversations with hurting people where the subject matter sprang from the problem of forgiveness.

We've seen the pain one lives with when he or she has been unable to forgive a parent for past hurts or when one spouse has held a past problem against the other for years. Trust and confidence erode; freedom and joy dissolve under the heaviness of the unresolved relationships. But with forgiveness comes freedom. We say with confidence that one is never closer to God than when in the process of giving and receiving mercy.

8. *When conflicts are handled properly, everyone grows.* Insights are exchanged; truth is discovered; we learn more about one another and what is truly important. More than anything else, conflict can reveal what is deep within us: what we care about most of all, what has hurt us, what we believe in. As these sorts of subjects boil to the surface, relationships advance in quality and help us grow.

The man who prayed that the lion chasing him would turn out to be a Christian misunderstood something important: Being a follower of Christ does not preclude conflict. Being a follower of Christ should make a supreme difference in how one handles conflict, however.

When true Christians conflict, they are simply communicating at the deepest possible level. If they do it as if Christ were watching, the conflict can turn into a growth experience. The fact is that Christ *is* always watching.

Gordon: *My father told me a story that has had great influence on me. In his younger days, he frequently became quite combative in conflict. Then one night he had a dream where he was giving a talk to the church. As he talked, he expressed strong, even hostile feelings to the congregation. One by one, the people got up and began to leave the room. In his dream, my father asked one of the older men in the congregation, "Why are they leaving?"*

"Because," came the answer, "the people refuse to listen to an angry man."

Gail: *Well, Gordon, you learned that lesson well, because I have watched how carefully you avoid needless conflict.*

Gordon: *You have, have you? How do I do it?*

Gail: *Often you say things like, "Now I could be wrong, but. . . ." and "This could be my fault, but. . . ." or "Tell me if my perception is inaccurate, but this is what I'm hearing." That opens the door to dialogue instead of conflict.*

Gordon: *People often get angry when they feel their selfhood is being attacked, so if you can keep a conflict from straying into areas where a person's well-being seems to be threatened, you may be able to resolve the issue.*

Gail: *But it doesn't always work that way. Sometimes people look at every conflict as a personal battle. They may angrily win the battle and lose the war.*

Gordon: *That's what will happen if intimacy is wounded beyond repair.*

WITHOUT
EMPOWERMENT
The

Heart

Cannot

Be

Touched

11
Building People

Gordon: *You're going through pictures of the kids again.*

Gail: *Sometimes a mood comes over me, and I just have to stop and remember when the kids were young. Still like this one of the two of them?*

Gordon: *It's a favorite. Why do we both keep on doting on this particular shot?*

Gail: *I'm not sure. I find myself staring at it like I do when I'm staring into a fire.*

Gordon: *I'll never forget that dress Kristy used to wear. She was a princess. How old were they when this was taken?*

Gail: *Umm, I think she's two, and that would make Mark about five.*

Gordon: *You can almost see the man starting to come out in him. I love the way he holds her hand so firmly and then raises his other hand.*

Gail: *Almost like a policeman saying, "Stop! This is my sister, and we're coming through. I've got everything under control."*

Gordon: *Sometimes he was a tease and a provoker, but most of the time he tried hard to be her friend and ensure that she was included in whatever was going on.*

Gail: *He was proud of her. He wanted her to meet his friends, do what they were doing, and share in the fun.*

Gordon: *I think he did that because she always made it clear that she believed in him. She was there cheering at his games, and she was there to give him a boost when things didn't go right. She could get him to talk about things that I'm not sure we could have gotten out of him. It was special to watch the two of them.*

Gail: *They built a sister-and-brother intimacy that made our home a real delight.*

Gordon: *I guess that's what you call empowerment.*

We weren't aware that this particular picture had any special meaning for Mark, now married and a father himself, until we listened to him speak to a group of theological graduate students about the quality of life in a pastor's home. When quizzed about sibling relationships, he remembered the picture and described it to the students. Then he said, "the only regret I have about my relationship to my sister is that I wish I'd held her hand more like that while she was growing up."

This was Mark's way of reflecting upon a principle of relationship that has been very important in our home and our friendships. We call it *empowerment*. Some might think of that as a business term, but it's more than that. It's a word that describes how people concerned about intimacy offer one another care, encouragement, and the space to grow.

Even though Mark told the students that he wished he'd held his sister's hand more, the truth is that he did a more than adequate job. Like him, Kristy is also married and often expresses her admiration for the way her brother walked through early life with her.

We weren't always sure that was what he had in mind when, as a child, he would defeat her mercilessly in games where physical strength could easily prevail. Even then, he seemed to bring a sort of healthy toughness out of Kristy. It came in handy when she later had to cope with teenage society. As the two entered the maelstrom of adolescence, it was a great comfort to us when Mark invited his sister into his circle of friends and helped her build credibility with the crowd. As the older brother, he certainly held her hand and introduced her to his version of growth. The two of them forged what we call an empowering relationship.

Empowering has to do with the investments people make in one another. It is what happens when we concern ourselves with the question, Is the person with whom we are friend, spouse, or family a growing person because he or she is in intimate connection with us? The empowering issue is one of contribution: what kind, how much, and to what purpose?

Jesus had this empowering principle in mind when He called upon the disciples to love one another as He'd loved them. They would become the most impressive products of His empowering efforts. When you take a quick look at those men who later became the apostles of the Christian church, their transformation over a period of only a few years is nothing short of remarkable. That transformation was largely due to their intimate relationship to the Lord.

Simon Peter is the foremost case. He traveled a long distance, growth-wise, from life as a fisherman on Lake Galilee to life as a missionary apostle in Jerusalem and other parts of the world, but the growth journey was the product of the empowering efforts of Jesus.

How did Jesus shape Simon Peter into the man we ultimately know him to be? It seems to have all begun with an invitation and promise made by the Lord: "Follow me, and I will make you. . . ." Peter's transformation took place as he was able to watch Jesus closely: how He lived, what He said, the way He handled critics and detractors, the choices He made under stress. Jesus was transparent with Peter.

But don't forget the Lord's sensitivity to Peter. He honored Peter's dreams and desires, knew where this diamond-in-the-rough man needed to grow, helped him name his weaknesses, and provided him with insight into his human potential. Jesus knew Peter fully; He looked deep into his life, much further than anyone else had ever bothered to look. It's clear that Jesus knew Peter better than Peter knew Peter.

Don't forget communication, either. The record of the conversations between the two is instructive. There are insights, rebukes, encouragements, warnings, and conflicts. Study the words and you begin to sense that, from the very beginning, Jesus had a God-designed purpose for Simon Peter. He was preparing or empowering the man to become an innovative leader of the earliest band of Christians. That empowering activity created an intimacy of amazing proportions.

One watches Jesus patiently oversee a dramatic transformation of Peter, a process not marked by intimidation, threat, or the imposition of conditions. Rather, Jesus created a unique growth environment, an empowering environment, one in which Peter could grow freely, stretch to the maturity of apostolic character and God's special purpose for his life. When there was failure of any kind, Jesus was always there to pick up the pieces and graciously assist Peter back to wholeness again. Again, this is what intimacy is about.

One of the unique messages of the Bible is the value of the person and the clear proposition that there is a purpose of divine origin and significance embedded in each life. Each person is as distinctive as a snowflake; each is endowed with an unusual constellation of gifts and capacities, insights, and observations. But each person needs empowerment in order to grow to the fullness of this embedded purpose, and that is the ultimate design of a relationship: We are meant to participate in the bringing of each other to maturity. We empower each other to grow.

Exactly how does that happen in human relationships? Let's try a metaphor that may provide some understanding.

When it is gardening time each spring, the man or woman with a green thumb heads for the soil. Dirt is turned over, mixed with some fertilizer, and furrowed for seeds and plants. A successful gardener will be generous with time, energy, and resources. The objective is a garden where everything is free to grow to the fullness of its potential for food or beauty.

You have to know when the tomato plants need to be supported with stakes, how much sunlight the beans and peas will need, and the room the cucumbers will need in order to spread out. That's care!

You have to spot the weeds before they take over, outfox the sneaky animals who like your plants as much as you do, and maintain a careful watch for insects. That's protection.

The gardener has to enter the garden every day in something of an empowering mood. That's faithfulness! You can't make plants and flowers grow; you can only provide them with a better-than-average opportunity. That's patience! Do your job right, and things come to full ripening and flowering at just the right moment. That's the blessing.

The empowering environment in which Peter matured was enlivened with kindness and grace. Was Christ ever more gracious and kind to anyone than He was with Simon—especially in the tough moments when Peter utterly fizzled in his attempts to be Christlike.

When someone acts graciously or kindly toward another, he is choosing to give that person not what he deserves but what he needs. Nothing produces intimacy faster and deeper than choosing to act in this fashion.

Few people needed that gracious sort of relationship more

than this one particular disciple. We're talking about a man who could be reckless, impulsive, and abrasive. It took a lot of grace to nudge him toward growth. Many of us would have blown him off, and Simon Peter would never have achieved greatness.

An empowering environment where people are free to grow includes several different elements. The first of those elements is patience.

Empowering One Another Requires Patience

In human relationships, people who empower others are always, first of all, patient people, and patience is a quality that often seems to be in short supply.

In a world where things such as jets, computers, FAX machines, and satellite communications create something of a sense of instancy, we can easily lose sight of the significance of patience. Who likes to wait for anything anymore?

We demand change in one another—maturity, adult responses—now. We are just as likely to be impatient with ourselves. "If I can't change this habit, beat this addiction, alter this attitude, lose this weight by tomorrow evening, it's probably not worth the attempt."

Simply put, patience is the willingness to generously give another person time and space to grow. Patience means we downsize our expectations, our timetables, our methods, and permit God's purposes to prevail. Patience does not demand; it lovingly waits.

We've heard our friend, Dr. David Seamands, tell of a woman who once acknowledged that her impatience with her husband had often caused her to act as if it were her responsibility to change him. She later learned that "it was my job to love him and let God change him." According to Seamands, the change in attitude worked.

Jesus Christ displayed remarkable patience, not only with Simon Peter, but with all the disciples. When many of us would have been tempted to write them off because of their stubbornness and resistance to truth, Jesus stuck with them, giving them time and space to develop.

Watch the patient Jesus each time His men showed weakness or naiveté. He didn't overreact to their panic when a storm became treacherous and events were beyond their control. He only asked a searching question: "Where is your faith?" He didn't publicly embarrass them when they failed to know what to do with a demon-possessed boy. He only gave them a simple lesson: "This sort of thing cannot happen without prayer and fasting."

Patience is the lubricant of relationships. It is what stops heat from building up when someone we know begins to rub us the wrong way. When there is stress in a relationship, patient people do not instantly lash out. First they ask themselves, *How is he or she seeing this issue? Why would someone choose to say or do things that way? What causes such anger, hurt, or enthusiasm?*

Patience is in evidence when we act in sensitivity and attempt to take into account the stress or the blind spots of others. If we understand what they do not see or something of the pressures they are facing, perhaps we will come to a new and better interpretation of their actions.

How often each of us, in a desperate moment of inadequacy or shortcoming, has silently begged for patience from others. We want to cry out, "If you only knew how tired I am, how pressured I feel, how much hurt there is in my life, how dumb I feel." We desperately hope that those in our circle of intimacy will understand and offer us a second chance.

Then there are those moments when another needs our patience. Here is the acid test of our ability to act within the circle of intimacy. Will we be as quick to be patient as we hoped others would be for us?

Many times a person has no idea that he is creating certain impressions or inconveniences for others. In such cases we may speak of blind spots. "He just doesn't understand what he's doing," we say. "He's got a real blind spot when it comes to that." Sometimes the person in question is not prepared to face up to the exposure of a blind spot at that moment. In an intimate relationship, there must be enough patience to wait for a good teaching time. "I could not feed you with meat," Paul said to his immature friends in the Corinthian church as he waited for the right moment. "I had to offer you milk as one offers it to babies" (*see* 1 Corinthians 3:1–3). The man was being patient.

By no means is patience to be mistaken for compliance. It is not that we are simply ignoring another's immaturity or irresponsible behavior; it is a matter of knowing that every one of us has a personal growing season.

Nor is patience to be mistaken for co-dependency or what is sometimes called enabling. These seem to be some of our culture's latest "buzz" words. When a member of any family or group is addicted to a substance such as alcohol or a life-style such as workaholism, the tendency for others in the circle of intimacy is to adapt to that person and his behavior by denying the facts or trying to minimize the embarrassing consequences. They think that what they are doing is a show of patience. It isn't. Protecting the addict, accepting undeserved blame for what he or she has done, denying the reality of irresponsible behavior simply isn't patience. Unfortunately, it is a reinforcement of bad behavior, and the end result is a continuation of a worsening situation. Everyone involved

best, the second-in-command. They wanted to get His
mpliance on their decision to tell a nondisciple to cease and
sist from delivering people from demons. They wanted His
thorization to destroy a small town by fire from heaven
en they were refused hospitality.

Why put up with men like that? Jesus knew what they were
become, and that caused Him to be gracious and bear with
eir momentary childishness. He stuck with them.

In his book *Spiritual Leadership* (Moody, 1980), J. Oswald
nders notes a revealing comment by J. Hudson Taylor con-
rning his relationship to the men and women around him,
o often seemed to slow him down, rather than make his
y easier. "My greatest temptation is to lose my temper over
e slackness and inefficiency so disappointing in those on
om I depended. It is no use to lose my temper—only
ndness. But oh, it is such a trial."

Difficult as it may have been, Taylor did keep his temper;
was patient with those who were not traveling at the speed
in the direction that God was leading him. Without such an
ement of graciousness, the people around him would never
ve developed and been able to carry on the Taylor vision
ter he was gone. Every relationship needs patience like
at, even if it is painful in the early going.

Empowering One Another Means Offering Protection

an empowering relationship, patience has to be augmented
ith another quality of grace: protection.

When you look at Jesus' friendship with the twelve, you
n see all sorts of occasions where He stepped in and offered
word or mounted an effort that prevented them from facing
e full consequences of their silly mistakes or immature

sinks deeper into anger, becomes isolated and al
co-dependent relationship begins to destroy e\
path. Patience is a restraint that occurs in the lig
change and growth; co-dependence is a denial
even a problem.

David took great comfort in his relationship \
he was reassured that God was looking over him
who "has compassion on his children . . . for he
we are formed . . ." (Psalm 103:13, 14 NIV). Dav\
in the relational patience of his Heavenly Father
knew that God was not expecting more of him
capable of giving at that point in his growth proc

The phrase, "He knows how we are formed,
King James Version puts it, "He knoweth our fran
God is patient with our development. And that I
lot to us. We never wanted our children to be any
than what was mature for their age. When our da
twelve, we delighted in her normal behavior as a t\
old. We would have been alarmed if she had tried
or seize the privileges of an adult. We would ha
discipline only if she had acted like a six-year-old.

In the same way, God is patient with us. He isn't
spiritual performance from us that is out of line wit\
we have been following after Him. He is patient;
our frame—its evil propensities, how much stress i\
the extent of its possibilities. And when we came
stand that truth, the patience of God helped us rela\
comparing ourselves with other Christians who were
us or behind us.

Can you imagine the patience demanded of Jesus
disciples, after considerable time with Him, came t\
three successive occasions with petty attitudes and p
They wished to know who among them was to be co

choices. We can see how Jesus was constantly breaking the trail in front of the men who followed Him, particularly for Peter.

Peter could manage a fishing boat or a seafood outlet without too much trouble, but confronting evil, healing people, and preaching the kingdom was another story. Although he was definitely drawn to the task Jesus laid before him, Peter nevertheless seems to have managed to make every mistake that could have been made. If he was to be empowered, he would need protection from his own compulsions and from the consequence of his blunders until he reached some level of godly character.

In intimate relationships there is such protection. Paul used the word *forbearance* to make this point when he taught people how to get along with each other. The word conveys the sense of shield or shelter. You see a small child seeking this kind of forbearing safety when he or she becomes frightened of a stranger's attempt to play. The child withdraws to its mother, may wrap his or her arms around mother's legs and seek assurance in the touch of her body.

To differing extents, that sort of covering or shelter is an indispensable element of every relationship. Jesus seemed to do that for Peter with great frequency, and if He hadn't, Peter probably would have (to use a modern idiom) shot himself in the foot more than a few times.

Take the time, for example, when Peter asked to join Jesus, who was walking on the water (Matthew 14:28). The Lord assented and beckoned him forward. Everything went fine until Peter apparently became confident of his own agility. He immediately sank, becoming the fool.

We might have been tempted to allow Peter to sink a little deeper and choke a bit before the rescue. Not Jesus. He offered a hand immediately, pulled Peter up, and walked him to the boat. Peter never mentioned the incident again, but he must of thought about it often. Interestingly, Jesus never mentioned it again, either.

We offer a protective hand when we hold one another accountable for right behavior and good choices, when we recognize that we can make a terrible mistake by not challenging one another to higher levels of life.

Protection means loving someone enough to poke underneath the surface and call attention to the signs that suggest a destructive problem may be on the way. Not to do that suggests that our love is not very genuine and our relationship is something less than intimate.

What are we to do when someone fails? Like Peter, they would sink to the bottom, unable to save themselves. Empowering protection may mean the necessary covering that provides the sinker with time and space to find healing and redirection.

Paul had this sort of grace in mind when he wrote to the Galatian Christians about "sinking experiences" and challenged them to undertake a protective act he called restoration: "If someone is caught in a sin, you who are spiritual should restore him *gently*" (Galatians 6:1 NIV, emphasis added). Gentle restoration means protection in the form of helping to put the pieces back together again.

When Paul wrote these words, he was concerned about people who might have committed serious moral or ethical errors. The usual reaction in many relationships would have been to dismiss such people from the congregation or simply ignore them, dropping them from the circle of friendship.

We have seen examples of this when people go through the tragedy of a marital breakup. A woman who recently went through the experience of divorce told us:

When it became public that my marriage was breaking up, many of my friends just seemed to disappear. It hit me that if I'd lost my husband through death, they might have crowded around me with things to do and places to go. But losing my husband through divorce meant that these same people tended to abandon me and take away the privilege of doing many of the things that would have brought meaning and stability through my time of grief.

The person who loses a job sometimes discovers that friends offer condolence and support for a few weeks, but as time passes, they withdraw more and more, leaving one alone when a steadying hand is needed the most. "I guess I just don't know what to say to him when I see him coming," an acquaintance says, trying to explain the neglect. Perhaps there are times when words are less important than the quiet hand that pulls one out of the sinking condition.

Protective intimacy means that although there may be no answers, people still come close and stay near.

We have a vivid memory of a major emergency in our family life. Kristy, when only two years old, was rushed to the hospital because she had taken a drink of turpentine. Some of the medical personnel who worked on her thought we might lose her. Others were concerned about brain or kidney damage. We felt as if we were sinking to the bottom as we sat there in the waiting room absolutely helpless. We shall never forget the sudden sense of buoyancy we felt when several men and women from our congregation came to sit with us. Their presence was the hand of Jesus reaching out to us in our sinking state. They had no answers to offer, nor did they have any way of making the situation more promising. All they had was that steadying hand that offered protection from fear and dread.

Jesus' protection of Peter was never more evident than on the night of His betrayal and crucifixion. In front of all the other disciples, Peter was prepared to stand and pledge his ultimate love for Christ. He was ready, he said, to die for the Lord. Of all those in the group, only Jesus appreciated how futile Peter's words were, how inadequate his will, and how soon the promise would be broken.

It would have been a human reaction for Jesus to have ridiculed or at least rebuffed Peter that night. Rather, Jesus offered a pointed but gentle warning of what was about to happen: "Simon, Simon, Satan has asked to sift you as wheat. But I have prayed for you, Simon, that your faith may not fail. And when you have turned back, strengthen your brothers."

But Peter persisted. "Lord, I am ready to go with you to prison and to death."

Jesus' sad response was: "I tell you, Peter, before the rooster crows today, you will deny three times that you know me" (Luke 22:31–34 NIV).

Protection bonded with patience produces love like that which Jesus showed Peter that night. Someone else would probably have said, "Peter, you've had three years to come to your senses and three years to face up to your impulsive mouth, but here you go again. We're going to have to find someone else with more class and character."

But Jesus didn't say that, and that is the kind of love He was calling the disciples to show one another in the years to come. You have to believe that Peter often looked back on that evening, awestruck at the magnanimity of the Savior.

In one "Peanuts" cartoon adventure, Linus found Lucy in one of her crabby moods. Then he saw Charlie Brown headed in their direction and knew that the two were apt to bring out the worst in each other if they met.

A lesser person might have been tempted to stand back and

enjoy the fireworks, but Linus seems to have a protective nature. He stopped Charlie and said, "When Lucy's crabby like this, everybody should be warned to stay away from her." Then, to Charlie's amazement, Linus went to where Lucy was sitting in silence, "crabbiness" written all over her scowling face, and began to encircle her with emergency road flares. This was Linus's way of protecting Charlie and others from needlessly experiencing Lucy's wrath. At the same time, Linus was protecting Lucy from showing a side of herself in need of containment. He stuck with her when others would have walked out of her life.

Jesus stuck with Simon Peter at his worst moments. Paul tells us to stick with a stumbling Christian. The Bible calls us to offer steadying hands to struggling, vulnerable people in our world.

One of our nineteenth-century heroes is Charles Simeon, vicar of Holy Trinity Church in Cambridge, England. He wrote:

> I consider love as wealth; and as I would resist a man who should come to rob my house, so would I a man who would weaken my regard for any human being. I consider, too, that persons are cast into different molds; and that to ask myself, what should I do in that person's situation, is not a just mode of judging. I must not expect a man that is naturally cold and reserved to act as one that is naturally warm and affectionate; and *I think it a great evil that people do not make more allowances for each other in this particular* (emphasis ours). (Quoted in *Charles Simeon of Cambridge* by Hugh E. Hopkins, Eerdmans, 1977.)

Jesus made enormous allowances for Peter, knowing that in just a matter of weeks, this fallen soldier would become a powerful preacher, a marching general, through the fullness of the Holy Spirit. That night Jesus empowered Peter to carry on toward that destiny by protecting him from the folly of his momentary weakness. Patience and protection. Without these elements in a relationship, there can be no intimacy. Without them, no one grows.

Gordon: *I have been drawn to that conversation between Jesus and Peter over and over again.*

Gail: *It really has become very personal for you, hasn't it?*

Gordon: *It really has. Having experienced failure that became very public and very humiliating, these lines have meant a lot to me.*

Gail: *What is it in particular that hits you?*

Gordon: *Well, I wince at Peter's inability to know himself and his foolish claims about courage. But I think that what really catches my attention is Jesus' perspective on Peter's upcoming bad night. The Lord looks straight through Peter's blasphemous denials, straight through the stunning defeat, beyond the tears, and into what Peter is going to become.*

Gail: *The Lord hasn't given up on him.*

Gordon: *No, Peter may be a fallen soldier for a moment, but he will be a marching general soon.*

12

Keep Building

Gordon: *It's been years since I lived with migraine headaches. Remember? I'm sure glad that's over.*

Gail: *I have a vivid recollection of the nights you had pain that seemed unmanageable.*

Gordon: *The headaches were that and more. But something powerful came out of that experience. Prayer! The migraines opened the door for us to learn how to pray together. Perhaps I should say that they opened the door for me to pray with you.*

Gail: *Praying together is such an important facet of intimacy. It's surprising that it took us so long to see its importance.*

Gordon: *It wasn't your fault; it was mine. A lot of men simply find it difficult to pray with their wives in a natural way. They don't mind doing it at the dinner table or at general family functions. But really praying together about people, events, fears, and dreams? That's another story.*

Gail: *Why do you think that's true?*

Gordon: *I think it has something to do with transparency. Most men are taught never to show weakness, and prayer is certainly showing weakness and dependence. Prayer places us in a posture of vulnerability. We feel strange confessing, and asking, and speaking in a subordinate relation-*

ship, as you have to do when you address God. But that's a thing many men have to overcome.

Gail: *And the headaches? How did they affect this fear?*

Gordon: *When you get into such pain that you're desperate, you'll try anything. I remember one evening when I was ready to tear my head off and I asked you to lay hands on me and pray for me.*

Gail: *That was the breakthrough, wasn't it?*

Gordon: *Once it finally dawned on me that this praying together was a great comfort, that it was not a threat to my manhood, that it brought us closer together and closer to God, I was ready to pursue a mutual prayer life. But you have to be transparent to people for that to happen.*

Gail: *I rank that breakthrough as one of the most important events of our marriage.*

When we look at that special picture of our two children when they were young, we see one of Mark's hands grasping Kristy's, while the other reaches forward as if to protect. One day he would realize that there is another direction for a hand to reach: upward.

The Empowering Relationship Requires Intercession

Relationships that enable people to grow have to be marked with intercession, the prayer one makes on behalf of another. Intercession is the act of standing between someone and God in order to bring them together. That was what Jesus had in mind on that crisis-laden night when He said to Peter, "I have prayed for you." Peter often seems to have been the object of intercessory prayer.

As a leader of the church, Peter found himself in prison one

night, while the enemies of the congregation were trying to stamp out its leadership. "But earnest prayer for him was made to God by the church." Before the prayer meeting ended, Peter was miraculously released from prison and stood pounding on the door of the very place where the prayer was being offered for him. The intercessors were incredulous when they opened the door and found him standing there—so incredulous, in fact, that they left him standing there while they debated as to whether or not it was really him. That was intercession with great effect.

All relationships will be relatively shallow until intercession is included in the empowering environment. We must learn how to hold up one another before God.

The most magnificent example of intercession in relationships is seen in Jesus' great prayer for the disciples.

> My prayer is not that you take them out of the world but that you protect them from the evil one. . . . Sanctify them by the truth. . . . My prayer is not for them alone. I pray also for those who will believe in me through their message, that all of them may be one. . . . Father, I want those you have given me to be with me where I am, and to see my glory, the glory you have given me because you loved me before the creation of the world. . . . I have made you known to them, and will continue to make you known in order that the love you have for me may be in them and that I myself may be in them (John 17:15–26 NIV).

Jesus' concerns when He prayed for His friends were that they would know victory, unity, and joy; that they would experience protection from the enemy; that they would pursue holiness and thereby be equipped to undertake their tasks to God's glory.

How many intimate friends and spouses do any of us have

whose prayer we can count on? Probably not too many. Perhaps we could enlarge that number if we courageously initiated the element of prayer in our friendships, our marriages, our families. The keeping of prayer lists and checking up regularly to see how God may be answering prayer are all parts of building intimacy.

One thing we've discovered that deepens a friendship is to make sure that we follow through on a promise to pray. When we commit ourselves to intercede for people, we put their names in our Bible and try to pray for them every day. It's important to check back with them to find out how they're doing and how we can sharpen up our prayer request. Second, we like to drop them a note, not only saying that we're continuing to pray, but adding a portion of Scripture and a few sentences of the prayer we're praying. People are greatly helped by such concern.

After many years of noting God's responses to our prayers for our friends in our journals, we have a host of reminders that He does hear and answer prayer. To be sure, the answers are not always as we would have wanted, but over time, we've seen some amazing results. Few things have meant more to us than the privilege of praying for our friends.

The Empowering Environment Demands Forgiveness

When we talk about the "grace environment" as part of empowerment in relationships, we need to recognize another element that Jesus provided His disciples: forgiveness. Without it, no relationship can last for very long, yet all too frequently, this is a missing element in the pursuit of intimacy in marriages, families, and friendships.

Early in His public life, Jesus made the giving of mercy a

major issue. He was thinking about it when He talked of the state of heart and mind one brings to worship. He warned His listeners never to come to the altar until they had scanned every personal relationship to ensure that all conflicts had been resolved (*see* Matthew 5:23, 24). That included the granting of forgiveness. There was no place for any hint of bitterness or resentment at the altar, as far as the Son of God was concerned.

Judging by their actions, many Christians do not seem to believe that He was serious. It is not unusual to see men and women coming to worship with their marriages in a state of brokenness. Nor is it unusual to take note of believers sitting near each other in the sanctuary when they haven't spoken for long periods of time because of unresolved conflict. Many people do not seem to believe in the importance of forgiveness as a key to healthy, empowering relationships.

Jesus not only taught forgiveness, He modeled it. After their embarrassing betrayal of Jesus, the disciples experienced three days of what must have been total gloom. That misery would have continued, had it not been for the resurrection. The good news was that Christ was alive; the question was, how would Christ respond to their pathetic loss of courage on the night before the crucifixion? Among the very first words sent from the risen Savior to the disciples were: "Go tell the disciples and Peter. . . ." Peter knew Jesus was still talking to him.

Not long afterwards, there was the emotional reunion on the shore of Galilee (John 21). The depressed Peter and the others had spent a fruitless night on the lake, and when day broke, they saw the figure of Jesus beckoning them to a breakfast He'd cooked for them. As the men gathered around the fire on what must have been a chilly morning, the message

was obvious: The Savior had chosen not to hold their dismal performance against them.

Think of it: the Son of God cooking breakfast for forgiven men. It was a magnificent picture of healing.

Forgiveness means deliberately choosing not to hold something against another when an injury to the relationship has occurred. Some say that forgiving is forgetting, but that is a rather frustrating concept, since most of us are too human to forget. It is more accurate to say that although we may not have completely forgotten, we have chosen to give what is needed—mercy.

Forgiveness is not only an action in relationships; it becomes a life-style. As we practice not to react immediately when someone does something that offends or hurts us, this response becomes a way of life. We begin to take on the attitude Jesus assumed at the cross, when He prayed, "Father, forgive them; they're ignorant of what they're doing."

As a merciful Person, Jesus assumed that the actions of many of the angry people at the cross were done in blindness and ignorance. He chose to show regard for the evil in their hearts that would instigate such an injustice as His crucifixion. That was Jesus' manner all through His public life. If He showed anger, it was never toward a person but rather at the sin within that caused the person to act the way he did. Being able to separate the sin from the sinner is the first step in being able to live in constant forgiveness.

Lewis Smedes has written powerfully on the subject of forgiveness. He suggests that there are three things that must always take place if offenses are to be wrapped in healing mercy.

First, he writes, when we are wronged, we must frankly face the effect of what has happened. If we have been hurt, let us admit the fact to ourselves. Joseph was wronged by his

brothers on several occasions, but when he met them as prime minister of Egypt, he showed that he had chosen not to hold their actions against them. "You intended to harm me," he told them, "but God intended it for good." That closed the books, as far as Joseph was concerned.

Joseph was not in denial over what had happened. He had experienced all the possible consequences of their jealousy and anger, but having faced it, he was ready to get on with life.

Smedes suggests that a second aspect of forgiveness is an act of spiritual surgery upon ourselves. In forgiving, we determine to slice away the wrong act someone has done and, at the same time, recreate in our minds a new view of the wrongdoer, as if he had never done the original deed. That is a courageous thing to do, and it demands the power of Christ at work in us. It is, in fact, what Jesus Christ was doing in the prayer of forgiveness on the cross. He was seeing those people through forgiving eyes, as if they had never perpetrated the act of crucifixion at all.

Then Smedes proposes that he who would forgive start over. Reconciliation is a personal reunion of two people who were alienated but belong together. It is not excusing the wrong, nor even forgetting it. It is choosing to free oneself from the past and look to the future.

That is exactly what becoming a forgiving person makes possible. The one who forgives is released from the past, freed to seize the present and the future. What is sadder than the person who carries a load of bitterness and self-pity from wrongs done to him in the past? Though he may be a talented, attractive person, he rarely engages in relationships that could be called empowering relationships, because his unforgiving mind is too much on himself and the past. He is nailed to the past, and no one grows in the presence of such a resentful man or woman.

Paul was cruelly beaten and imprisoned in Philippi. He had every reason not to want to return to the town or have anything to do with the Philippian jailer who'd made his life so miserable. But because he could forgive by putting the past behind him, a church was raised up in that community—one that became his favorite. The Philippian believers were enabled to grow in relationship to Paul because he followed what would become the Smedes formula of forgiveness.

Some of us find forgiving more difficult than others. We may hold grudges for long periods of time, want to win conflicts, justify or protect ourselves, and resent it when we lose. We may carry pockets of volcanic anger within, which are set off any time we are reminded of issues and struggles of the past. No intimacy in marriage, family, or other quality relationship can exist as long as these tendencies go unconfronted and unresolved.

Although it may be a dramatic spiritual and emotional challenge, those of us possessing such tendencies must face up to the reality of our unforgiving spirits if we ever hope to be part of a gracious environment in which others can grow.

Gordon: *I have been on both ends of forgiveness. I have had to forgive, and I have needed to be forgiven.*

Gail: *It's probably not healthy to dwell on such times too long, but I recall both occasions. I remember when a person had disappointed you so deeply that you couldn't get over it.*

Gordon: *So much so, I finally had to face the fact that I had allowed myself to fall into feelings of outright hatred. For weeks, I lingered in that state of heart, with a crippled spirit. I remember crying out in desperation to God for deliverance. The answer did not come easily. But one* *afternoon I had what seemed to have been a mystical experience. As I acknowledged that I was guilty of hate and needed release, the freedom to forgive suddenly came. But I had to relinquish all rights to get back at the other person. And I had to promise God I would never couple this person with the incident again. Talk about the experience? Yes? Name the person? No.*

Gail: *And that ended it.*

Gordon: *Yes, it did, and I'll never forget the moment which followed that surrender. It was as if a hole were cut in my heart, and hate drained out of my chest cavity. Instantly, I felt ten pounds lighter, and the days that followed were among the most fruitful and satisfying I've ever had.*

Gail: *What do you think would have happened if you hadn't passed that crisis?*

Gordon: *I think I would have spent years in spiritual paralysis. But I also have to mention that I have known the necessity of repenting and asking forgiveness from you and from others. When a person has to do that, he has to renounce all rights to excuses, defensiveness, and rationalizations. And he has to simply say, but it is not really simple, "I am utterly wrong. I need mercy." Today, I feel as if I walk in mercy, and not because I have to keep asking for it. It was given, and the issue has been closed for a long time now. But I never forget that the most intimate relationships I have are there because of mercy. I would never, never take that gift for granted.*

Gail: *Gordon, I'm sure you remember a woman who, when we first met her, was going through a painful divorce. Her husband had left her for another woman, and she had to face the fact that she was going to be left with two young boys, little if any financial income, and lots of loneliness.*

Gordon: *When we first knew her, she seemed far too mild and weak*

> *to survive the pounding she would have to take as a single parent.*

Gail: *Yes, and I can remember the awful sadness as I went with her to court when her divorce decree was finalized. We wept together over the financial frustrations, over behavior problems, and over her concerns about the future.*

Gordon: *And sometimes we wondered what kept her going.*

Gail: *Well, one of the things that kept her going was her ability to forgive her ex-husband. She followed Lewis Smedes's recipe for forgiveness completely. She faced up to the pain in her life but refused to grant herself needless pity, much less seek it from others. She also took a look at her ex-husband and mentally managed to separate him from his sin. She saw him as a sad and misguided man rather than someone out to hurt her. And that meant there was never any attempt to slander him before others for the purpose of giving him a bad name. Finally, she kept a picture in her mind of what this man could be if he ever came to the realization of the way he was running away from God and his responsibilities.*

Gordon: *For years we have watched her maintain that spirit, and today both sons are adults, college graduates, and married.*

Gail: *And they are a real delight to her. She still has moments of loneliness and inner anguish, but her ability to forgive has saved her from being a bitter and unhappy woman.*

The Empowering Environment Demands Investments

When our son, Mark, turned sixteen and began to drive the family vehicles, he approached his father with the question of whether he could use our pickup truck for a big Friday evening date.

Not only was he relatively inexperienced as a driver, but the date was in the heart of Boston, and the drive into the city would be made at the peak of rush hour.

"Son, let me think about your question for a couple of hours and then get back to you," Gordon said. We talked about it and decided that, although there would be two nervous parents throughout that evening, it was time to trust our son's judgment.

Two hours later, father and son talked again. "I've decided that you can use the truck on Friday," Gordon said, "but on one condition."

"What's that, Dad?" Mark asked, obviously ready to agree to anything.

"I want to drive the entire route with you the day before, at the same time of day. What's more, I want you to demonstrate that you know how to handle any situation you might face."

"No problem, Dad," Mark responded.

On Thursday night, Mark and his dad started driving north on I-95 to pick up I-93, which would take them into the heart of the city.

Traffic was moving slowly when Gordon suddenly said to Mark, "Son, you have a flat front tire. Did you know that?"

"No, I didn't, Dad," Mark answered. "There's nothing wrong."

"You didn't hear me, Bud. You've got a flat tire because I said so. Now let's move over to the side and change it."

When they were parked on the side of the freeway, Gordon got out and sat on the guardrail. Mark came around and said, "What do you want me to do?"

"Well, if I were your date, I guess I'd want you to do whatever is necessary in order to change the tire. And I'd want you to get started, because it looks like rain is coming."

Shaking his head in consternation because the front tire

looked just fine, Mark crawled under the truck to find the spare tire and jack. A few minutes later he crawled back out from the rear of the pickup and said, "Dad, where's the jack?"

"I'm your beautiful date, son," Gordon responded. "I'm not expected to know where the jack is. Sounds like you've got a problem."

Mark continued to look—under the truck, behind the seat, under the seat. For ten minutes he searched for a jack he'd never had reason to locate before. Finally he found it under the hood, and before long he had the front of the truck up in the air. It was then that Gordon pronounced the tire whole again, and they started toward Boston once more.

When the two reached the exit ramp Mark was to take, Gordon informed him that the ramp was closed due to construction. "No, it isn't," Mark said.

"I just closed it," came the reply.

Mark had to find another way to reach his destination, without benefit of map or directions. When he did, they parked the truck in the parking lot and immediately exited, much to the surprise of the lot attendant.

On the way home, Gordon pronounced the alternator sick, and that forced the two men over to the side to discuss what one would do in such a situation. When they reached home, they had lots to laugh about.

But the next evening when Mark left on his big date, he drove off confidently. He had been empowered through his dad's investment of time and teaching. He knew how well he could perform in any untoward situation, and he knew he enjoyed the confidence of his father. He had proved himself, and both he and his dad knew what he could do. This intimacy between a father and a son was built on an empowering transfer of knowledge and the confidence to use it.

An empowering relationship flows like this: The elder leads

the younger, the stronger assists the weaker, the expert teaches the novice, the experienced shares with the first-timer. One pours into the other the knowledge and the confidence necessary for maturity and effectiveness. It is an investment of sorts, a transfer of resources that results in growth.

Little by little, Jesus invested in His disciples. In the early stages of their relationship, He simply invited them to watch. Then He asked them what they were learning. It was not long before He was asking them questions, making them think. Then there came the time for "trial runs." When they returned, He would quiz them closely, making necessary corrections and suggestions.

What was the aim of all this? It was preparation for the day when He would give His mission of world evangelization over to them. He not only expected to give it to them, He looked forward to the fact that they would do greater works and accomplish more than He had. That would be the payoff of His investment.

Empowering may be one of the most difficult challenges we face in relationships—giving our best to others and then watching them move out ahead to accomplish what we've helped them learn—perhaps even better than we can do it. This is the essence of what some call discipleship.

Affirmation

Affirmation is another type of investment present in an empowering relationship.

Earlier we saw an example of affirmation between the Heavenly Father and Jesus ("This is my beloved son in whom I am pleased"). The Lord gave many such examples to those who followed Him.

Jesus was quick to affirm Peter when he spoke boldly concerning whom he thought Jesus was ("The Christ, the Son of the living God"). Mary of Bethany was affirmed for choosing the priority of sitting at the feet of Christ, and Zacchaeus was publicly affirmed when he recognized and repudiated his formerly corrupt activities at the tax office in Jericho.

Affirmation is that act of identifying and ascribing value to things that others have done or could become. Few things in the empowering environment are more critical to intimacy. We see countless examples of people who carry hurt and anger with them throughout a lifetime because they lacked affirmation at critical times in their lives.

A friend of ours, Ken Blanchard, is well-known for his co-authorship of the best-seller *The One-Minute Manager* (Kenneth Blanchard and Spencer Johnson, Morrow, 1982). In the book a young aspiring businessman seeks out models of managerial style that would set him on the pathway to success. Finally, he is put in touch with a man nearby, who grants him an interview. Before long he is invited to tour the company and talk with people who work for his host. They share with him the key to their success. One of the essential ingredients is "one-minute praisings."

"What is a one-minute praising?" he asks. "Catch people doing something right," someone says to him. A one-minute manager, he is told, touches people, looks them straight in the eye, and tells them succinctly what was good about what they have accomplished and how delighted management is as a result. People will do almost anything to receive a one-minute praising, Blanchard claims.

The One-Minute Manager reflects a very obvious truth about empowering relationships: People grow by affirmation and praise. Perhaps it is a shadow of the praising we hope to hear from God when we appear in His presence someday. We all crave some significant individual to ascribe value to our person, our competence, our maturation.

All relationships thrive on affirmation, and when someone resists providing it, the relationship begins to hurt and generally never reaches the fullness of its potential.

We work hard at affirmation, especially through the sending of notes and cards. Whenever we see someone who is making a contribution that may go unrecognized, we try to praise that person through a thank-you note or a special word when others are present and can hear our expression of appreciation.

Milton Friesen was a friend who gave his life to street people in Boston. Down through the years, his efforts marked the lives of thousands. He seemed to have a boundless supply of compassion for people whose lives had collapsed.

One day it became apparent that Milton Friesen was a sick man and could be lost to us at any moment, so some of us who loved him dearly decided to sponsor an appreciation dinner. It was a smashing success. Person after person came to the front of the banquet hall to talk about things this man had done to show the love of Christ among street people in Boston.

One comment we will never forget came from a professional singer of classical music. Milton had asked her to come to Kingston House, his base of ministry, to give a concert for the men and women who came off the streets to receive a meal and a place to sleep. He asked her to sing some heavy classical music. "These are God's children," Friesen told her, "and I want them to hear the very best music possible." Her subsequent concert was Milton Friesen's way of ascribing value to his beloved street people. He was that kind of man— always seeking to affirm, always putting value on people in the most creative ways.

When most people make investments, they carefully project what business calls the ROI (return on investment).

That is not so, however, in the kind of investment one makes in empowering relationships, for when we empower one another, our investment is ultimately designed to give the ROI away. In other words, that which we build in the lives of other persons we finally release; we give it away. That is the third aspect of our investment program in empowering people.

Release

Parents invest in their children and then release them. In another sense, friends build in one another's lives, releasing each to the service and possibilities to which God has called them.

The opposite of release is possessiveness. Nothing is more ugly than a possessive relationship, where someone attempts to hold on to another. Growth is stifled; love turns into resentment, freedom into entrapment; intimacy grows cold.

Although the disciples were never more servants than the day Christ ascended to heaven, they were nevertheless released, freed to the even larger mission of world evangelization. Jesus had poured Himself into them through commitment, transparency, sensitivity, communication, and investment of all sorts. Now He set them free to make the choice to follow His Holy Spirit and preach the gospel, carrying on His redemptive mission.

That once-motley group of men, a strange mixture of subcultures, vocations, and political and social groupings, became the apostles of the Christian church. They changed the world. They were loved into an intimate relationship with Christ, and they duplicated that love for one another and others.

Sometimes it is painful to release one another. So many of us have our own little insecurities and want to hold onto what we've got. A mother wants to hold onto her son, a man to his business subordinate, a teacher to his pupil. A Christian discipler wants to maintain a grip upon a young believer, and a wife wants to possess all the time her husband has to give. But all come to realize that the more they are willing to release others to the impulses of the Holy Spirit, the more intimacy they, the "releasers," are likely to enjoy. That is one of the strange paradoxes of Christlike love. Of course the principle works when all the other elements of a healthy relationship are in place, also.

A classic story demonstrating this release is the life of Eli, the high priest of the tabernacle in Shiloh, and Samuel, the young man whom he raised for Hannah and Elkannah. One night when the boy rushed to his bedside thinking that Eli had called him, the old man had to face the fact that Samuel was hearing God's voice. Although some might have been tempted to jealously conceal the fact, Eli told Samuel what he suspected. It was God speaking, Eli told Samuel, and if the voice was heard again, Samuel should answer it in a particular way.

You can't help but wonder if Eli felt a bit of pain that Samuel was receiving God's special attention instead of him. Why the younger rather than the older? But Eli released Samuel to become exactly what he had trained him to be: a man in touch with God's heart. That was Eli's return on his investment.

The picture of our young son and his little sister will always be a precious possession for the two of us. Each time we look at it, we see the figure of two human beings locked in a relationship—in this case, brother and sister. With a grip on her wrist with one hand and giving a gesture of direction and determination with the other, he seems to be saying, "This is *my* sister, and I'm going to make sure that she gets where she's supposed to go." He got her there, and his investment paid off.

When a friend, a spouse, a parent, or a mentor decides that another should be empowered to become all he or she was designed by God to become, watch out for progress, watch out for growth. It will come, and a little part of the world will become a better place. Intimacy will have happened.

Gordon: *I remember when my father taught me to ski. We took a rope to the top of the practice slope. When we got ready to go down the hill, he had me position myself between his skis. Down the hill we went, very slowly at first. His hands were on my hips, guiding me along, teaching me how to lean, transfer my weight from ski to ski, in order to make the proper turns. When necessary, his knees pressed against the backs of mine, showing me how to bend and swivel properly. By literally being pressed against his body, I picked up the natural movements of skiing quite quickly. With each right movement, he would shout encouragement, and at the bottom of the hill he would tell me what I did correctly or incorrectly. As we went down the hill again and again, I could feel him letting me drift progressively farther from him. Then came the moment when he released me to ski ahead while he stopped and cheered. "Go ahead, son," he shouted. "You're on your own."*

Gail: *I know you had your share of falling.*

Gordon: *Oh, yes. In fact, as soon as I was left on my own, I fell. But we started again, and it wasn't long until I was indeed totally on my own, skiing crudely, but nevertheless skiing. Not too many days later, I was skiing with my father on the better slopes, keeping up with him, thoroughly enjoying myself. That's a good picture of empow-*

190

erment: guidance, constant affirmation, and final release.

Gail: *Another thing I have learned about empowering is that it never happens when one party in a relationship assumes he has nothing to learn from the other. One of the keys in our friendship is that you have taught me and also have allowed me to teach you.*

Gordon: *You have taught me people skills.*

Gail: *And you have taught me how to study the Scripture and how to teach. Perhaps what I find most amazing is that you as a preacher have allowed me to use stories and quotes from your notebooks.*

Gordon: *But remember, you can't use them within five hundred miles of anyplace I'm going to be speaking.*

Gail: *Well, that's only fair, I guess. But the point is that we each brought value into our relationship and by God's grace have transferred it to the other.*

Gordon: *We've seen far too many marriages where one person assumes the other has nothing to teach him or her. In my pastoral counseling, I find that one of the common characteristics of failing marriages is the husbands or wives could not accept advice or guidance from their partners. In many cases, there was a jealousy of what the other did well.*

Gail: *Why do you think so many husbands and wives don't feel they can learn anything from someone who loves them?*

Gordon: *Maybe it's because we fear showing weakness or inadequacy. To permit ourselves to be taught is to say, "You know and can do certain things I need. Help me!"*

Gail: *It takes some maturity to say that, doesn't it?*

❧

IF

THE

HEART

IS

NOT

TOUCHED

Then

There is

Nothing to

Celebrate

❧

13

Celebrating Intimacy

Gordon: *Every time I drive on this freeway, I have flashbacks to my college years.*

Gail: *Why here?*

Gordon: *Well, see that empty building over there? That's where the trucking company I used to work for was located. It's hard for me to believe that I worked there for two years, five nights a week, from eleven in the evening to seven in the morning.*

Gail: *Every time you mention your trucking days, you refer to the loads of explosives that were parked in the yard each night. Is that the place?*

Gordon: *We were always transporting dynamite for road building and mining in the mountains.*

Gail: *Weren't you ever nervous, knowing there was enough powder outside to send you to the moon?*

Gordon: *That's putting it mildly. We made sure those trailers were parked in a restricted place. Then we put large lettered signs on all sides that said "Danger, Explosives." No one but authorized personnel could come near. We wouldn't allow any smoking. You couldn't take too many precautions.*

Gail: *Have you ever thought about the fact that those explosives, when used properly, could be a vital asset and when used improperly could be your worst enemy?*

Gordon: *We used to talk about that a lot. We'd say that with dynamite you can either build a beautiful road or cause a lot of damage.*

Gail: *The whole issue of sexual intimacy is like that.*

Gordon: *Just like dynamite, you're saying.*

Gail: *Exactly. Pursue sexual intimacy in the proper way, and it becomes one of the most wonderful dimensions in life. Abuse it, and it can explode in your face and create havoc you won't believe.*

Gordon: *I don't think you could have found a more apt metaphor. It's dynamite, all right. Friend or enemy: our choice. Depends on how we decide to use it. I am well acquainted with the pain of its misuse . . . as well as the pain it causes others.*

In 1987 we went to Switzerland in an effort to put distance between ourselves and a very sad time in our lives. For a month we walked together in the Alps and immersed ourselves in some of the world's most beautiful scenery.

In a book entitled *Keep Climbing*, Gail has written about one of those days when we set out on what we anticipated to be a simple trek through an Alpine valley to a place the map called the Strela Pass. When the walk gradually evolved into an unexpected strenuous climb, we talked about turning back, but doggedly kept on climbing. Eventually, we made it to the top.

What compelled us to keep on pushing ahead (and up) was a mixture of raw determination, magnificent scenery, excellent weather, and well-marked pathways. After six hours we reached the Strela Pass, but not without sore feet and one bloody knee. Once there, we were consumed by a common desire to drop where we stood and sleep forever.

Though we didn't sleep, we did sit at the top for a while. We talked about the steep ascent to the Strela Pass and how glad we were that we had persevered. There we came up with the idea of Gail's book and decided it had to be called *Keep Climbing*—which is exactly what we'd done in the previous hours.

We also spoke of other things: about coming back someday, perhaps bringing some of our friends who would love this place as much as we already did. We talked about the satisfaction of accomplishing difficult things and how this climb would be a future inspiration to us when we might be tempted to quit other more significant challenges. It was an intimate occasion, a celebration of joint accomplishment mixed with feelings of exhaustion and exhilaration.

An enlarged photograph of the instant we reached the Strela Pass hangs in Gordon's office. We stand together in its foreground. Behind us you can see the speck of a town where we'd had breakfast early that morning and enthusiastically made plans for a leisurely hike. The picture shows the pathway we took, as it snakes through the valley and then begins the sharp unanticipated climb up the mountainside.

To get us both in the picture, we placed our camera on a rock, set the timer, and then rushed to a spot twelve feet away. We struck the most valiant pose we knew, held our breath to stop from shaking in fatigue, and waited for that distinct shutter noise that assured us the moment had been captured on film.

The photograph on Gordon's office wall is very important to us. It symbolizes our own intimate life together, the dimensions of which we've tried to describe in this book. It reminds us of the many years we have stuck to each other in marriage and partnership. And stuck we have, through times when it was easy to stick because life seemed so perfect and through times when life's events turned so dark that we doubted the possibility of a bright tomorrow.

Today, when we look at that picture, we can trace the narrow path we once walked in the valley. We can remember the place along the way where we flopped in weariness and engaged in brief conflict over quitting the journey. We can see the spot where we stopped and drank cool water from a mountain spring. And there, further along the trail, is the point where Gail slipped and fell and we feared for a moment that she had injured her knee.

Since we met no one during the upper stages of our climb, we assumed that we were the only people who had decided to make the Strela Pass their mission for that day. The mountain was ours, we thought, and this experience of being on top belonged to no one else. But we were wrong! Very wrong!

As we left our resting place and began to walk through the pass to the other side of the mountain, we suddenly heard music in the air. Then, as we came around an outcropping of rock, we spied people—not just a few people, but crowds of people, hundreds of people. Some sat drinking beer, some were dancing, and some were just strolling about, posing for pictures on the deck of a huge mountain restaurant. We were anything but alone! This was like rush hour in New York City, except for the dancing.

Where had all these human beings come from? Surely they had not made the same exhausting climb we had. At least we hadn't seen them on the way up. When we drew closer, we could see there were no indications that they had recently pushed themselves to the physical limit of fatigue, as we had—not a laughing, dancing, picture-taking crowd like this one. They were engaged in pure frolic; we, on the other hand, could hardly move.

Then we learned the secret. These many hundred fun seekers had ascended the mountain from the other side, not on foot, but by mountain tramway. All it had cost them to get to the top was a dozen Swiss francs and twenty minutes of their time—no work, no sweat, no exhaustion! They were enjoying the same scenery it took us six hours of work to enjoy, the same sense of relaxation and enjoyment at the Strela Restaurant, the same memory of being at the top. To us it seemed quite unfair. We felt robbed, even a bit foolish.

The climb to the Strela Pass is a parable of sexual intimacy, for what two people experience in a sexual union can be likened to an experience at the summit—exhilarating and renewing pleasure at the end of a long ascent.

But remember, in the parable there were two kinds of climbing, one made by a couple who paid a heavy price to reach the top, another made by a large crowd of people who paid a small price and rode by tram, in ease and comfort, to the same place. At the summit, both had similar experiences of seeing the scenery, enjoying the mountain air, and recording a rhapsodic occasion on film. But while the surface experiences of the two may have been similar, there are important differences, and it is that difference that defines genuine sexual intimacy.

Instant Replay

Let's review our conversation when we first reached the top. When we plopped down and rested that day in 1987, we carried on three kinds of conversation. We talked first about the climb itself and—as we often do now when we look at the picture—we pointed out the places where we had walked through the valley and where we'd climbed the steep slopes. We remembered then, as we do now, the tough spots, the resting places, the points where we'd measured our progress and the distance still to go.

At the top, there was a second kind of conversation. We talked about how proud we felt of each other and how glad we were that we had kept on climbing when more than a few out-of-condition midlifers like ourselves would have found it easy to turn around and go back. We thought aloud about how the climb had required a common commitment and what we'd learned about the value of frequent encouragement.

There was a third conversation as we pondered the horizon behind us on the other side of the Strela Pass. After all, having done this, we were now ready for the next challenge. Tomorrow, perhaps. During the steeper parts of the climb, we had thought seriously about not doing this ever again, but that was *before* the summit. We saw things differently at celebration time. Now we were prepared to take on the whole of the Swiss Alps. Summit experiences do that for climbers.

These are the sorts of things that sexual intimacy is meant to do for people when they've reached the "summit" *under proper conditions*. Intimacy in the sexual moment is an indescribably wonderful human experience that physically, emotionally, mentally, and spiritually builds on three perspectives: looking back down the slope to recall where we've come from (the past); looking at each other to affirm how we perceive our mutual covenant (the present); and looking to the horizon to renew the intention to journey further on together (the future).

In the active sense, sexual intimacy involves a set of gestures—touching, stroking, embracing, joining, and talking—which are meant to be pleasurable to the senses, revitalizing to the emotions, definitive for the mind, and focusing to the heart.

These are, of course, the most personal of human gestures. In a nakedness that has and should have no shame, we offer our bodies to each other in order to give and receive pleasure. If we are obedient to God's laws, we give ourselves to our marriage partner in a way we would give ourselves to no other person.

If you stop and think about it, all relationships—from the most intimate to the most casual—are symbolized by certain unique gestures. Some of these gestures vary from culture to culture, and one has to be careful that he or she learns the appropriate gesture for each relationship, lest there be misunderstandings and embarrassments. Within each culture certain gestures send a message about the relationship they define, a message concerning the appropriate quality and depth of intimacy.

The Japanese bow when they encounter each other. The bow is a message of respect. Beyond that, one can discern who among those bowing is the most revered, for he will receive the deeper bow from the other. This bowing and knowing how deep to bow is no small thing to Japanese people as they seek to define and symbolize their relationships.

As we said in an earlier chapter, a handshake is a gesture with a message. Once upon a time, it meant that the extender of the hand was not concealing a dagger or any other weapon. It sent the signal that there was no immediate danger. As the centuries have passed, the handshake has taken on a more positive meaning, and we have come to recognize differing kinds of handshakes.

There is the stiff, formal handshake that is usually the sign of a first-time meeting or the mark of civility between diplomats. There is also the traditional, hasty, good-sport handshake between two boxers who, at the sound of the bell, are about to try to pound each other into the canvas. There's the warm, prolonged handshake of two old friends and the two-handed shake (accompanied by a nanosecond of eye contact) often employed by politicians in search of votes. Then there is the lingering handshake of a man and a woman who are exploring each other's eyes for signs that romantic possibilities may lie ahead. This leads to hand-holding, which is the next step beyond handshaking.

The gesture of embrace is an acceleration of intimacy. For example, two Latin friends vigorously hug each other, slapping backs with enthusiasm. Lovers who are now well beyond the stage of hand-holding cuddle tightly. Then there's the quick squeeze of father and daughter, the affectionate fondling of mother and child.

We know what these and other gestures mean. They send a signal of closeness, a sense of warmth, an assurance that there are no conflicting issues. They say peace and love, all is well. They say that two people are on a converging track of deepening relationship. In the parent–child exchange, there is even more, perhaps: reminders of protection, bondedness, of earlier moments when an infant nursed at a mother's breast.

But sexual intimacy is the greatest and most intense of these dramatic gestures. Such intimacy does more than signal no danger, as a handshake does, and it does more than signal enthusiastic friendship, as in the Latin embrazzo that draws another close. Sexual intimacy dramatizes connectedness, "one flesh," two people who have chosen to become one in spirit.

While many people of the Christian tradition have found it difficult to talk openly about sex, the Bible does not. Any Bible reader knows passages that are quite candid about the sexual behavior of men and women. We read of married couples exultant in the ecstasy of sexual passion and the conception of children, and, on the darker side, of lust, adultery, rape, sexual perversion, prostitution, homosexuality, and incest. We read the mysterious poetry—some would call it erotic—of the Song of Solomon and conclude that the players in these chapters are enraptured with the anticipation and the experience of sexual play, and they show no reticence in expressing their feelings. Nor is the biblical writer reluctant to expose the reader to these frank poetic lines. The Bible is anything but halting in addressing all of these sexual matters and the good or not-so-good repercussions that abound as a result.

Neither is the Bible remiss in saying to the reader that there are specific conditions under which God the Creator condones this most dramatic of all intimacy gestures. There are serious consequences for those who violate God's law; there are great rewards promised for those who keep them.

We grew up in a period when people did not speak of sex as openly and candidly as they do today. Most parents communicated these topics to their sons and daughters with awkwardness, if at all. In the church, sexual intimacy—its meaning and conduct—were spoken of in vague generalities and religious code words. Unfortunately more emphasis was placed on the forbidden aspects of sex and the many ways one could fall into sin and perversion. Fear of dreadful consequences, of being humiliated and ostracized, of disease, of life-long shame were often associated with sexual topics, and as a result, any sense of the beauty and joy of sexual intimacy was usually buried in the stern admonitions and warnings.

With tongue in cheek, Charlie Shedd probably described the religious mind-set of the age well when he opined that if the minister and wife had children, people assumed they came through artificial insemination or the immaculate conception.

Good people enjoying sexual intimacy simply seemed incomprehensible.

Because the two of us believed that a fulfilling sexual relationship was of paramount importance in our marriage, we determined to break from that mold. During our engagement, we asked lots of questions of older people whom we thought might be helpful to us. We read everything in the Christian and non-Christian literature that was recommended, and we talked together about what we were learning and what we anticipated. These were among the most enjoyable and anticipatory conversations of an engaged couple who had kept themselves "virginal" until marriage. The result was that when we came together on our wedding night, we were probably as ready as it was possible to be where there has been no previous sexual experience.

We quickly learned, however, that all the reading and questioning never quite prepare a man and a woman either for the magnificence of sexual experience or the great potential there is for misunderstanding and conflict. This, quite truthfully, was an area of life that was dynamite: capable of making the best of things to happen or capable of being unbelievably destructive.

As we sought to learn the fullness of the summit experience in sexual intimacy, we were impressed with how helpful the biblical literature was in laying a groundwork for thinking and conviction.

For example, we saw how the Hebrew portions of the Bible, when translated into English, offer three verbs to describe sexual activity.

The verb *to lay with* is most often (but not exclusively) used to describe sexually active people who are violating the laws of God. Potiphar's wife, attempting to seduce the Hebrew Joseph, says "lie with me," and one gains the sense that this is sexual activity for nothing more than the pleasure produced when two people lie together and engage in genital stimulation.

A second verb, *to go into*, is used when the biblical writers describe the intent of a man and woman to conceive a child. Now the carefully chosen words remind us that physical coupling—penetration—is necessary for conception. It is not that there is an absence of bliss or affection in this act, but it is clear that procreation is the central purpose the couple had in mind, when this verb is used.

The third of the Hebrew verbs is translated *to know*, and it elevates the intent of sexual intimacy to a new height. To know includes the meaning of the first verb (that two do lie together), and it contains the meaning of the second verb (that penetration does occur), but it goes on to add a third and most significant premise: that in such intimacy two people are pursuing and enjoying emotional, intellectual, and spiritual knowledge of each other. They are one!

Earlier in this chapter we emphasized that at the top of the mountain we had three kinds of conversation. We looked back to the valley and recalled where we'd walked; we exchanged words of endearment and enthusiasm for each other and this shared accomplishment; and we renewed our desire to press on to other horizons. It is this same sort of thing that happens when a man and woman, committed to each other in love, embrace in the sexual intimacy of the marriage bed. The implication is that there are three kinds of "conversation" in that moment, also.

Recalling the Recent Journey

The celebration of sexual intimacy is made possible by a look back "down the slope" of recent living. Meaningful "knowing" is made possible by a recollection of recent acts in the relationship where commitment, transparency, sensitivity, communication, and empowerment have been taking place.

The authors of books on sexual activity often bypass a significant element in the pursuit of ultimate sexual satisfaction when they limit themselves to describing only those physical gestures that bring a person to orgasm. Pleasurable feelings there certainly may be, but full satisfaction that reaches the soul and spirit, leaving no guilt or emptiness in the aftermath, comes only when foreplay includes the words and acts of the previous hours, where intimacy has been acted out on all levels of relationship.

Those who do not understand this are often confused when after a day or evening of neglecting their marriage partner or carrying on in conflict, they do not find him or her ready for sexual expression when the lights go out. They are ignorant of the fact that the memory of insensitive words, the absence of affirmation or attention, or the carelessness of abrasive behavior leaves another in no mood for the "knowing" of sexual intimacy.

In the initial days of our marriage, we had to learn that every sexual experience could be described with one of the three biblical verbs mentioned earlier. Clearly we were not interested in only the first verb (laying with). We were not prepared, in the earliest days, for the result of the second verb (to go into), unless God willed otherwise. But we were desirous that our sexual intimacy be that of "knowing" each other, that highest and best experience that includes the best that all three verbs imply.

That meant careful preparation and attention to the quality of life in the hours *before* it was time to meet in the marriage bed: sharing responsibilities in the home and in the relationship; maintaining a flow of affection, appreciation, and sensitivity for each other's needs; being quick to resolve conflicts through patience, confession, and forgiveness.

It meant asking questions such as: Is there authentic peace in this tiny world of ours? Does the record of our behavior in common endearment show that we truly are one? Because if there isn't; if there is only a recall of hurt, confused or angry thoughts, there may later be a physical experience of sex (laying with or going into), but it will not be intimacy; not the *knowing* of which the Scripture speaks so plainly. All of these issues are a significant part of what some call foreplay.

Renewing the Solidarity of Vows

The second of our conversations at the summit also has something to teach about sexual intimacy, for there were those moments when we were simply delighted that we were together, and that we had made this difficult assent ourselves. Such a sense of delight demands expression. We were kids again as we exchanged high fives. We hugged and kissed like two "happy campers"—make that climbers.

In the marvelous moments of sexual embrace, there are similar joyous expressions. We are saying, as we meet in the marital bed, that we have climbed today, and together we have reached another mountaintop in the journey of our lives. Just the two of us. There is none other who can share this moment.

In this hour there are words of recommitment, appreciation, and assurance of love. There is a kind of remembering that one day, years ago, we stood in front of a pastor, our families, and our friends and committed to each other. Now in each other's arms, years after that ceremony, each seeks the promise of the other that there will remain a specialness and uniqueness to what we are continuing to build in life. Each revitalizes their belief in the command of Scriptures that we should be willing to die for each other.

"Husbands, love your wives just as Christ loved the church and gave himself for it," Paul wrote to the Ephesians. This was not an insignificant instruction to Christian men who had just emerged from paganism and lived in a long tradition most poignantly expressed by Demosthenes: "We (men) keep prostitutes for pleasure; we keep mistresses for the day-to-day needs of the body; we keep wives for the begetting of children and for the faithful guardianship of our homes."

To die for each other, to give oneself to another, is a long, long way from Demosthenes' perspective on intimate relationships.

Reaffirming the Next Step

Then there is a third conversation held at the summit that reminds one of sexual intimacy, for from the experience of "knowing" comes a renewed personal determination to go on together: The future is ahead. What to do with it? Attempt more climbs? Live with the risk of more bloodied knees? Expect more exhaustion? But always knowing that, as a result of taking the next steps together, there will be more vistas to see and more summits to conquer, side by side!

Where does all of this end? There is a fresh gladness that we are together and an expectation that tomorrow will be better. Failures and disappointments of the past are put aside, lovingly forgotten. The "new" is upon us; the record is clean; what is most important is where we go from here.

We mean no arrogance, but as we stood together at the Strela Pass and surveyed the many hundreds at the Strela Restaurant who delighted in being at the top, we both knew there was a difference between them and us. Theirs was a summit experience bought with Swiss francs, not with the hard work of the climb. We had a memory of a struggle; they did not. We felt our position at the top was paid for not by money but by determination and grit. Somehow we knew that our time at the summit was of a different quality than what they were experiencing.

Sexual intimacy can be counterfeited—easily. Like the ride to the top of the mountain on the tram, two can pursue a sexual summit experience with no sense that there are commitments to make, none of those things reflected in our first conversation—that elongated period of foreplay, none of the second conversation—the reveling in commitment and endearment, and none of the third conversation—the anticipation of the tomorrows as lives grow closer.

Anyone at the summit can see the same scenery, whether they climbed for six hours or simply rode in the tram for twenty minutes. And anyone who engages in sexual activity with another can experience the same intense feelings for a few minutes, whether they have lived in intimacy with the other for weeks and years or picked each other up in a bar two hours previously. But the qualitative difference of the summit experiences is quite obvious.

Sexually speaking one has to do with the biblical concept of "knowing"; the other only that of "lying with." "Knowing" fills the inner parts of a person with a sense of confidence, of belonging, of being valued and cherished. "Lying with" leaves a person empty, devoid of value, feeling used, loneliness that is crippling to the soul.

Only obedience to God's laws constrains a person from seeking a superficial experience of intimacy with a sexual partner. We are long past the point in western society where sexual promiscuity is considered shameful by the majority. Various birth-control devices have removed the fear of untoward, life-altering consequences if one wants to live beyond the bounds of moral propriety.

A kind of everybody's-doing-it mentality has subtly reduced much of the effect a person's conscience might provide in the way of sexual discipline, and the pressures of modern life have caused people to feel lonelier, more alienated, and hungrier for intimacy. All have increased the barrage of sexual temptations, from pornography to prostitution, infidelity to homosexuality.

Today the horrifying and tragic effects of the AIDS virus are forcing some to reevaluate these tendencies toward what some have labeled sexual freedom. But fear alone—whether the older fear of pregnancy or the new fear of infection—is not going to cause people to think biblically about the meaning of sexual intimacy.

It is likely that such thinking will only occur when one turns to the One most supremely revealed in the Bible and asks what He calls upon men and women to be and to do when they choose to follow Him. The biblical standard concerning sexual intimacy is clear and nonnegotiable: Sexual love between men and women belongs in the confines of marriage. There it is a dynamite that completes the beauty of intimacy. But outside of it, sexual activity can become a dynamite that destroys and leaves little but misfortune.

❧

BUT WHEN
THE HEART
IS TOUCHED
There is Intimacy
And we begin
to discover
Why God made us
And how He desires
To have Intimacy
with us

❧

14

The Days We Remember, and the Ones We'd Like to Forget

Gail: *Look what I found.*

Gordon: *Looks like a stack of old letters.*

Gail: *Don't you recognize them? They're letters you and I wrote to each other while we were engaged. Do you realize you wrote to me almost every day for four months?*

Gordon: *I had to write. We couldn't afford phone calls unless it was something really important.*

Gail: *You read some of these now, and you can see how we were trying hard to reach into each other's minds to figure out what we were thinking about each other.*

Gordon: *I can't believe I wrote some of these lines. This is incredible mush!*

Gail: *Why don't you try writing some of those mushy words to me today?*

Gordon: *I don't have to write them anymore; I just say them.*

Gail: *I think a woman likes seeing them on paper, too.*

Gordon: *Look at this letter. We really were asking each other hard questions, weren't we? We had incredibly high expectations for a marriage.*

Gail: *We were probably a bit naive. We had no idea where these many years would take us, and the journey has had its difficult moments. But look where God has brought us to today.*

Gordon: *I really, really like where we are today. There's no one with whom I'd rather have made the journey.*

We need to share something with you. Years ago, we both committed our lives to what we call biblical living: the belief that the Bible is the Word of God to all peoples, that in it are the words of eternal life, and it contains all the directions and promises any person needs in order to fully live the life the Creator intended us to live.

One does not study biblical living for very long before making a couple of observations. First, the God of the Bible is a God of intimacy. He has willed not only that human beings find intimacy—connectedness—with each other but that they find supreme intimacy with Him. A God who "wires" His people to be capable of intimacy is a God who is intimate Himself, and it only makes sense that He would provide ways in which intimacy between heaven and earth could be experienced.

We also observed that the Bible confronts its readers with some outstanding personalities, the ultimate of which is Jesus Christ of Nazareth. The rest of the biblical players were ordinary men and women like us, but Jesus was God in the flesh. He came modeling and offering a new version of life to all who would follow, a pattern of living that can be summed up in one word: love. This love results in intimacy.

As we have speculated on the models of intimacy, we have been impressed that there are parallel experiences between our intimate knowing of each other and our intimate knowing of God. The two experiences are remarkable reflections of each other, so much so, that it stands to reason that a spiritual enemy would make the effort to thwart our respect and appreciation of one in order to diminish the effect and enjoyment of the other.

The Parallel of Need

Many pages ago, this book began with a brief sketch of how we met. Then we were at a stage in life where most young men and women are more than curious about discovering the person with whom they might spend their lives. In those days a *need* to give and receive love generally took precedence over other needs. Thinking about those times, we often laugh together as we recount the numbers of men and women we both dated, hoping to find that correct combination of characteristics that would make it easy to love and be loved. We found that combination in each other, and one evening a small diamond ring became our symbol of a shared intention to forge a lifelong partnership of vision and love.

Intimacy with God, we found, develops along the same pattern. It ordinarily begins with some sense of spiritual curiosity, followed by a sense of *need*. Who is God? Where is He to be found? What difference would it make if I found Him? Would I be a better person if I knew Him? And what does it mean when one whose name is Jesus comes along and says, "I am the way, and the truth, and the life. No one comes to the Father except through me"?

We may have thought to assuage our need for God through a rigid code of personal ethics: being a *good* person, an exotic philosophy of life, or some sort of meditative discipline. But nothing quite worked.

The letdown came because we are relational and our inner aloneness needed a relational answer. Philosophy, religion, meditation, and ethics are not relational in the sense that they provide a complete experience for the inner person. They provide something to do, something to think about, something to believe in, but they do not provide relationship. Knowing Christ intimately does.

The Parallel of Commitment

Having found what we were seeking, we walked the aisle of a church and pledged our lives to each other. The words, the vows, those expressions of verbal *commitment*, were easy to say, although there was some nervousness. The simple declaration of the pastor—"I now pronounce you to be husband and wife"—required little cleverness or energy from him. Only the soloist and the organist seemed to have had a difficult task.

In spite of the simplicity of the event, something powerful and mysterious happened. A covenant relationship was made in heaven. We had come down the aisle as single people; we returned up the aisle as married people. A fully legal and viable relationship was now in motion. We were as completely married in the eyes of the law as any couple celebrating their fiftieth anniversary that same day. More importantly, we were married in the eyes of God.

The point of the wedding day was simple: We put our convictions on the line and crossed it. We stopped saying nice things about and to each other and committed our entire lives. Nothing was held back, absolutely nothing—no unread fine print, no loopholes, no conditions.

Our Christian lives had much the same beginning. Earlier in the days of our youthfulness, we took the time to seek out the implications of following Christ, and when the exploration was over, it needed to be culminated with a decision. In the same way that we made pledges to each other in marriage, we individually, on another occasion, made similar pledges to Jesus. Acknowledging our personal need to know God, we gave Christ the key to the doorway of our lives. We admitted an inner condition of sinfulness and our need for forgiveness and realignment with God, His Father. That spiritual experience may not be as easily marked for others, but it was for us. Finding wasn't enough. Talking wasn't enough. We had to cross a line, walk an aisle, if you will, and *commit*.

In that moment, a relationship of spiritual intimacy was born. In the wedding with each other; in that personal commitment to Christ, a relationship with God.

The Parallel of "Honeymoon"

Our wedding took place in Illinois. When we left the reception that day, we journeyed to a small town located by a lake in Indiana. We went there because a treasured older friend offered us her home as a place for an inexpensive *honeymoon*. While almost all newlyweds we know today seem to go to Bermuda or Hawaii, we went to Indiana. It was all we could afford.

During that honeymoon nothing seemed to go wrong. We were quite willing to proclaim to anyone who took notice that we were dedicated to each other, that our love was unbounded. We were probably quite foolish more than once in our public displays of affection and endearments, but honeymooners are generally oblivious to what others think, anyway. At what other time in life would we take delight in tin cans tied to the back end of our car?

Spiritual intimacy with God is usually marked with a *honeymoon*, also. Euphoria, relief, gladness, nothing-can-go-wrong, my life is changed! These are the moments of excitement that many Christ followers remember best. It's a new and impetuous love for God that is beyond belief or explanation, and those of us who have enjoyed both kinds of honeymoons, wish they might last forever. But honeymoons are at best only temporary interludes.

The Parallel of Facing Realities

Honeymoons do come to an end. When ours did, we came home to a tiny apartment with inexpensive furniture and less than one hundred dollars in our pockets. It was time to go back to work. Euphoria has to give way to *facing realities*. Day-to-day living deepens our relationship or destroys it.

The emotional euphoria of the honeymoon soon collides with what is. There are leaky faucets, unpaid bills, cars that won't start, bosses that intimidate, and sicknesses that are no respecter of persons, even lovers. There are the challenges of merging diets, bedtimes and rising times, parceling out the tasks of cleaning, laundering, shopping, and cooking. And there are the dissimilarities in personal habits: Who takes a bath or shower when? Who leaves the toilet seat up, and why? Who is responsible for picking up dirty clothing? Who is crunching their cereal too loudly? Who is going to rise first on a cold morning and start the coffee? These issues never arose during the engagement, at the wedding, or on the honeymoon. But they—or issues like them—arose fairly quickly after the honeymoon ended.

Like every couple, we remember stumbling over many of these situations. There were low moments when each of us was tempted to wonder if we'd made a good decision back there on that hot August day in Illinois when we'd said, "I do." Was the person who once stood at the altar in that magnificent tuxedo and that lovely white wedding dress the same person seven months later when times were tough? Were those promises to love and cherish for better or for worse really keepable when the worse came along?

But the more we worked at loving and knowing each other, the more our styles of life and our attitudes begin to change. We did learn to understand and appreciate each other's different ways of doing things. We now knew what to expect from the other in moments of crisis. We were becoming "one flesh," and life changed for us.

Those earlier days were the days of test. Was our intimacy based only upon the euphoric occasions, or did our pledge to climb the slopes of life together also extend to the many, many days when one simply has to be faithful to day-to-day responsibilities of life? We observed that those bonded only to a me-first perspective in life were soon bored, seeking a way out, but those who said, "We will keep climbing," simply kept climbing.

There are similar *realities* in one's life of following Christ. Can anyone convince the novice Christ follower that there will be tough times where being a child of God is both joy and hard work? Probably not.

He or she comes to realize that growing in Christlikeness—a major objective of biblical living—is not always fun and good feelings. Christ's pathway also leads through places where the scenery is not memorable.

There are the struggles in learning how to pray when one would rather permit the mind to wander or simply fall asleep. There are occasions when reading the Bible does not offer the amazing, scintillating insights that used to leave one breathless with discovery. And there are the experiences in which some fellow Christ followers become more of a bother than a delight. The programs of the Christian community can occasionally become exhausting and consuming, and one is tempted to wonder, "who needs this?"

But, little by little, we are changing. As we pursue intimacy with Christ, knowing what pleases Him, sensing His unconditional love for us, we are becoming more like Him. His fellowship, strength, and provision are available to us. This is reality, too.

Facing realities is not *boring*. It is in the day-to-day routines that one makes new discoveries, new friends, accumulates new learning experiences, develops wisdom and maturity. When a number of years have passed, a couple comes to this conclusion: Our intimacy has been forged *not* in the moments of spectacular experience, but in the countless minutes and hours of living in community with each other and in the larger fellowship of the extended family and other friends. For there we faced struggle, made choices, played, and did good things. And there we grew in our intimacy with each other and with God.

The Parallel of Conflict

All relationships inevitably reach moments of extreme duress. They write lots of books about these times. *Conflict*, major misunderstanding, clash of values, carelessness, and insensitivity—the list goes on. Where are the intimate words of endearment now? Are we acting as though we aren't married? Why these accusations, these chilly silences, those tears, the glares that substitute for hostile words?

Where is the love that carried two young people down an aisle and made the vows so easy to say? Why is it so difficult to objectively hear the other's opinions? Why does each feel a need to win, to prove themselves innocent? Why, why, why, we ask ourselves, are all those early intentions to build in the other's life, to seek only the best for each other, become dissolved in this anger which suddenly seeks to hurt and maim our intimacy? It is a mystery, and in it we find forces in ourselves that have never fully submitted to the vows and promises. It is very frightening.

Here it was that we had to learn the meaning of confession and forgiveness. Never go to bed angry with each other, a mentor to our relationship had told us. It made sense because she had said it and because the Bible taught it. We were generally successful with this principle, but not always. There were those miserable moments when we laid side by side, inches apart, in that marital bed, the site of so many other blissful moments of sexual embrace. But now in this moment we lay sleepless in our hurt and anger. We make sure that no parts of our bodies touch, and if the other moves, we tense up for fear that an errant touch will force conversation once again.

We lie there staring up at the darkened ceiling, knowing all the time that this spooky stillness can be penetrated instantly if only one of us will say, "I'm sorry." That's all it will take. The mouth opens, and the lips form the words, but there is no voice. The inner being still resents and rebels; it is not ready to capitulate with humility.

But when the moment comes, there is often a rush of energy to unpack the conflict. The "I'm sorry" is, or should be, followed by an "I'm sorry, too," and the ultimate, "I forgive you." A flow of tenderness ought to follow, bringing resolution to something that moments ago seemed so shattered. How do relationships make it if there is only stubbornness and a need to be right? How can there be any kind of intimacy if two cannot find a moment of contrition and brokenness in the arms of each other?

221

Years ago, in the wake of one of these tense moments, Gordon wrote:

> We two
> Brought to a junction of conversation
> Two glimpses, dimensions and feelings
> Of a single reality.
> Volume increased,
> Faces reddened,
> And for a moment
> We stood like gladiators
> Dueling to the very death.
> Integrity and dignity seemed at first
> To be at stake.
> But as we parried and thrust
> With reason, wit, and turn of words,
> A remarkable thing occurred.
> For our momentary distance
> Led us both
> To a new birth of understanding.
> For after we had confessed
> To the presence of spirits
> That had to win and always be right,
> And after we renounced the hold of
> Those unpleasant inner forces,
> And after we had each said,
> "I forgive you,"
> A remarkable thing happened.
> For out of argument came a polished
> Insight which we two now treasure
> And would have missed
> Had we been afraid
> To trust our friendship
> To a challenging conflict.

And so it is with one's ascending journey with Christ. There's that horrible occasion when we suddenly find that we have offended Him and His good name, and we act as unbelievers. Our soul is in *conflict*. The promises we made to be obedient to His teaching and example are broken. We do, or say, or think things of which we never thought ourselves capable. Suddenly the first love and the freshening of faith that we thought would be permanent are gone, disappeared, and it is, for a short while, as though we had never believed. This, too, is very frightening.

But the same contrition—the same admission of and sorrow for wrongdoing—can break down this wall, as well. In so doing, Christ renews our fellowship with Him, and we once again sense the former freedom to enjoy His claim on our lives.

The Parallel of Productivity

On two occasions in our journey together we brought children home, a son and a daughter. Pictures abound of those days when we celebrated their first smiles, the first time they turned over in the crib, the first words, and the first walk. Two children: the result of our ascending journey together.

All intimate relationships are meant to be *productive*. There is a synergy of sorts, and it has countless expressions. What we could never have accomplished alone, we accomplish together, and we do it better and more effectively.

We grieve over those people who align in relationship and say of their ultimate goal: We seek first to make each other happy. Not enough! There is a dimension of intimacy that is the result of productivity, of results beyond ourselves—contributions made, things accomplished that you have done together and given to the world around you as a gift. You have made a difference. Thinking such thoughts, there was no greater challenge for us than to give the world two responsible children who would be a positive asset to their generation.

Faith that has no goals apart from self-satisfaction and good feelings is not faith. It is not intimacy with God, for we have been made to be intimate with the One who has made us, and as a result to serve in our times. Be *productive*. "If a man remains in me and I in him, he will bear much fruit," Jesus said.

The Parallel of Failure

Lest anyone wonder if we have known *failure* on our journey together, the answer is, yes, we have! We speak with considerable expertise when it comes to describing the lowest of the low moments in a relational journey.

We know what it is like to feel as if the very fabric of the relationship has been torn to shreds. We know what it is like to wonder if there will be another summit to climb. And we know what it is to have to walk the longest journey to ask for forgiveness and to choose to give it freely and without condition.

Most importantly, we know that couples, no matter how wounded, can recover and live the restored life. That recovery may even offer a stronger intimacy, a more valuable intimacy than the one known before.

We are constantly being asked if couples who have experienced a tragedy such as infidelity can ever recover from it. The first part of our answer is a resounding yes, when two people seize the two grace disciplines God provided for people who fail: repentance and forgiveness. Retreat from either one, and there is likely to be no hope.

There is nothing (not anything) that can be said to justify unfaithfulness—the betrayal of vows—in relationships. Everything can be said about the wounds it causes, the people hurt, the trust that is usually forfeited. But something else can be said: When two people have experienced a terrible fall in the process of the ascending journey and choose to rise again and keep climbing, they have learned some things about grace and tenacity of commitment that makes their relationship stronger than ever.

This same healing experience that can restore intimacy between two who seek to refresh their love is also true in one's relationship with Christ. *Failure* is not the end for the Christ follower, either. For he or she who would come to the presence of Christ at any moment with a contrite and sorrowful spirit will know the restoration of Christ's power and direction. No one wanders so far away that they cannot be welcomed home to the place of the waiting Father and given the greatest gift in the universe: the loving-kindness of the Lord: *intimacy*.

Intimacy

When a man and a woman make commitment to each other, become transparent and sensitive, work hard to communicate their hearts and minds, and labor to empower each other to growth and maturity, they eventually take time to climb to a summit, and there alone celebrate the meaning of their journey. They meet in that place of privacy and quiet, and there they embrace, their bodies made into one, and they know each other in that moment of the pleasure of the senses, the emotions, the mind, and the spirit.

It is a moment sacred to the relationship, shared by no one else, talked about to no one else. It is theirs and theirs alone.

It is about recalling, reaffirming, and redirecting, and there is *intimacy* and renewal.

So it is when the Christ follower comes into the sacred moment with his or her God, whether at the eucharistic celebration, in the closet of prayer, or at a time of quiet retreat. There is a celebration, and the same recalling, reaffirming, and redirecting. We call it worship, and there is *intimacy*—renewal.

If all these things are true, and supremely true in the area of sexual intimacy—that the intimate walk of one person with another is an echo of the intimacy God seeks to have with His people—does it become apparent why the enemy of God would wish to reduce intimacy to an empty, cheapened, undisciplined experience?

If everyone can be easily lifted to the summit by tram, then who will wish to make the climb any longer? If intimacy can be counterfeited with frequency by those who can afford it, then why go the long way and pay the price that this book has described? If the moment of sexual embrace is a celebration and not a moment of carnality, then is it not plain why an antichrist culture will do all it can to minimize and "animalize" sex as a sacred matter? If God intended us to see Him in the family context—Father, Son, child, bride—doesn't it follow that these earthly "pictures" of family should be destroyed?

We stand at the summit. The climb has been long, and it has not been the simple thing we thought it would be, at first. Most of the climb has been a marvelous experience. We have laughed along the way, and we have stopped to admire the wildflowers and drink the cool water of the mountain spring. Here and there we have tried to repair the pathway and leave it more convenient for the next traveler. We have known the bitter moment of a terrible fall, but we have made it to the top, and here on top, we look at each other with joy. We know that there will be many other climbs to make and the risk of facing challenges we can't meet, but we are together. By God's grace, nothing will separate us until death. Committed, transparent, sensitive, always communicating, helping each other to grow—that's intimacy, and the heart knows it.

Epilogue

Gordon: *Has writing this book been a good experience for you?*

Gail: *Sure, it's been good. I always enjoy working on a project with you, and it's refreshed my memory in all the things we've learned over more than thirty years of marriage.*

Gordon: *We sure were naive thirty years ago, weren't we?*

Gail: *Of course. But how could we know what we know now if there hadn't been struggles, defeats, challenges, and the opportunity to learn some extraordinary things from remarkable people?*

Gordon: *When we first got together, I don't think I knew much about sensitivity. I really had to learn it the hard way.*

Gail: *I'm not sure I was prepared to be transparent.*

Gordon: *We were probably good at communication, though.*

Gail: *Better than average, but look how far we've had to travel on that one, Gordon.*

Gordon: *I do think we've learned how to disagree and resolve the hurts we've inadvertently caused. We certainly had to learn how to give and receive grace and mercy. We've become stronger because of it.*

Gail: *Then there's empowerment. What do you think?*

Gordon: *I think that may be the best of all. The energy and courage you've poured into me has been the major secret of my life. I'll never stop being grateful.*

Gail: *And celebration?*

Gordon: *Holding you close to me is as exhilarating today as it was the first time—the tenderness, the caring, the pleasure. It's better as we grow older.*

Gail: *Then I think we're finding it.*

Gordon: *Finding what?*

Gail: *Intimacy, silly.*

For several years the telephone companies have been urging us to "reach out and touch someone." The fact of the matter is that Jesus Christ was calling people to do the very same thing almost two thousand years ago.

It is instinctive for people to look for intimacy, but few seem to find it in satisfactory amounts, and that is tragic. In a world where so much attention has been given to communications and self-understanding, why do so many still struggle?

In the opening paragraphs of this book, we quoted from a piece of prose Mr. Bridge, a fictional Kansas City lawyer, prepared to send his young bride. But she never saw the words. The reader is never told why. But it would appear that he could not bring himself to express his heart's thoughts so openly and freely. What she never heard was this:

> Thou only hast taught me that I have a heart—thou only hast thrown a deep light downward, and upward, into my soul. Thou only hast revealed me to myself; for without thy aid, my best knowledge of myself would have been merely to know my own shadow—to watch it flickering on the wall, and mistake its fantasies for my own real actions. Indeed, we are but shadows—we are not endowed with real life, and all that seems most real about us is but the thinnest substance of a dream— *till the heart be touched.*

We have tried to explain how hearts can touch. It's not easy, not quick, not without some work, but they can touch. We have found that the touching of hearts happens most readily for ordinary people who choose to make Jesus central to their lives and relationships. That is what happened to twelve men who accepted His invitation to follow Him. There was every reason for their loyalty to one another to have shattered, especially after Jesus left them, but the tremendous and encouraging fact is that their relationships did not fall apart, but grew stronger. Why? Because Christ was at the center of their choices, their values, their commitments.

The insights we have shared have come out of our experience, but that is not enough. What has made the astounding difference and provided us the power to discover intimacy in our marriage, our family, and our friendship is the power of Jesus Christ.

"Indeed, we are but shadows—we are not endowed with real life, and all that most real about us is but the thinnest substance of a dream—*till the heart be touched.*"

We were but shadows until God breathed into us the breath of life and we became living persons. Then He engineered the great human connection: "The two shall become one," and humankind learned the greatest possibility there is: two hearts can touch. That's intimacy.

Discussion Questions

Chapter 1
What This Is All About

1. Think of the three people in your world who most characterize intimacy to you. What do you see in their behavior that marks them as intimate people?
2. Think of three people in your world who discourage intimacy (these probably should not be named in a discussion with others). What do you see in their behavior that makes this happen?
3. Can you recall a time in your life when an older person took an intimate interest in you similar to the story of D. E. Hoste and a young girl? (*See* page 19.)
4. Read Job 19:13–20. Describe an experience you have had or someone you know has had in which loneliness or a lack of intimate "connection" generated physical consequences. What could have been done to alleviate the difficulties in that situation?
5. Study Psalm 139:1–4, 23, 24, remembering there was a time in David's life (many believe him to be the author) when he tried to keep a secret from God and others (2 Samuel 11, 12). What changes in his life are these verses suggesting?

Chapter 2
How Do You Make Hearts Connect?

1. What themes do you hear in Gordon and Gail's opening dialogue? What are you hearing in Boone Pickens's comments about his marriage?
2. How do you respond to Larry Crabb's observation that we yearn for personal relationships? Discuss how this longing could cause fear and anxiety in a person who had a history of childhood emotional or physical abuse.
3. Have you ever seen or been part of a group of "bonded" men or women similar to the disciples? (*See* pages 29–33.) What effect did it have on you? What did you observe?
4. Reflect upon Jesus' challenge to the disciples in John 13:34. Is this realistic for men and women living on today's "fast track"? What alterations in life might be necessary in order to proactively live the words of Christ?
5. Review the five shattered relationships that resulted from Adam and Eve's willful choice. How do you see those "shatterings" affecting us today?

Chapter 3
Everything Starts With Commitment

1. Have you ever experienced a time when someone helped you to "breathe" or when you did the same for another?
2. How does Dr. Bettelheim's comment relate to your personal experience?
3. Reflect on Ephesians 5:25–27. In what three ways is a man challenged to echo Christ's treatment of the church in his marriage relationship?
4. Make an inventory of those who are most closely associated with you. Do you usually feel encouraged by these people to be a more highly committed person (to God? to

relationships? to servanthood?) or do you often feel discouraged?

5. How does the story of David and Lisa Johnson affect you?

Chapter 4
Intimate People Are Transparent

1. As you read Gordon and Gail's beginning conversation, what themes do you respond to?
2. Think of those you know who qualify as most "knowable." What traits do they have in common? List those traits that are generally seen among "unknowable" people.
3. Jesus said, "Oh, there is so much more I want to tell you, but you can't understand it now" (John 16:12 TLB). On what occasions would it be unwise to "tell all"?
4. Identify the different emotions Jesus reveals in the Garden of Gethsemane (Matthew 26:35–56).
5. Why do many of us find communal prayer so difficult?

Chapter 5
When People Show Only One Side

1. What kind of fears are people revealing when they are careful to show only the "good side" of their personalities to others?
2. When someone has abused our vulnerability in a relationship, what does it do to us? What does it take to rebuild the trust?
3. Read Nehemiah 1:3–7 or Job 42:1–6. What do these texts have to say to us about being consciously aware that we are by nature sinful people? Why do so many people have to be broken by sin's consequences before they come to this conclusion?
4. What are the benefits of transparency?

Chapter 6
Sensitivity: The Art of Looking Inside

1. How do you see sensitivity and transparency working together in Gail's recounting of her forgetfulness?
2. Try to recall a time during this past week when someone was sensitive to your concerns.
3. Read Luke 22:31, 32 and Mark 16:6, 7. Note how Jesus was repeatedly sensitive to Simon Peter.
4. What does Maggie Scarf's comment say to you personally?
5. There are some whose temperaments are not naturally sensitive or transparent. How do we build bridges of relationship between each other when this is true?

Chapter 7
Waiting for a Good Moment

1. As you scan the stories of Jesus' life, identify several occasions when you see Him modeling sensitivity.
2. The authors have suggested that there are five ways one might develop sensitivity. Which of these seems most important to you and why? Perhaps you can add to their list.
3. What does it mean to "wait for the right moment" before saying something that may be necessary but nevertheless painful? What might make that difficult for you? What is your instinctive response when someone says something painful to you?

Chapter 8
The Gift of Talking

1. What are the patterns of communication Jesus used in communicating with His disciples?
2. List the ways in which people communicate beyond talk-

ing. What have you noticed about the way friends and couples communicate in terms of body language, where they sit or stand, and so on?

3. How do you react to the possibility that some people live vicariously through TV sitcoms? If you saw this happening in your family, what would you do about it?

4. As you reflect upon the conversations you've had this week, what percentage of them do you think remained at levels one and two? What has the description of the five levels done for your awareness of conversation?

Chapter 9
Going to the Bottom

1. Reread the Carlyle story. Is he typical? What could have been done to encourage him into different behavior before this relational tragedy occurred? Is there anyone in your group who finds personal expression difficult? Is it possible for them to describe the discomfort they sometimes experience at such times?

2. Review the level four and five conversations in this chapter. Are they realistic? What would it take to pursue this level of conversation with greater frequency between friends and married couples?

3. Are there two people in your group who would be willing to "replay" a level 3, 4, 5 conversation that might have happened in their home or workplace this past week? Discuss the points at which this conversation moved to deeper levels. What brought it to its conclusion?

4. Read John 21:15–25. On what level are Jesus and Simon Peter speaking? Why was this necessary? What does this conversation tell you about the two men?

5. Read Luke 9:35. Think through the affirmation given to

Jesus: "This is my Son [belonging] whom I have chosen [value]; listen to him [competence]." What difference would it make to you to receive such affirmations? From whom? How would you like to receive them?

Chapter 10
When Things Grow Sullen

1. How do you evaluate the ways in which Jesus and His disciples experienced conflict? What can we learn from this?
2. How can constructive conflict deepen or enlarge understanding in a relationship?
3. Is it easier for people to conflict in a church setting or in a different kind of organization? Why or why not?
4. Make an inventory of the conflicts found in the Book of Acts and discuss their relevance for today. Do we see similar conflicts happening? Where and how do they get started?
5. Which of the eight principles concerning conflict do you find most challenging?

Chapter 11
Building People

1. Comment on those people (but not necessarily by name) who have been empowering to you and say why. Where do you think you have been an empower-er? How do you think you've accomplished this?
2. In what ways does Jesus illustrate the principles of empowerment in the life of Simon Peter?
3. St. Paul comments that we should "consider the patience of Jesus Christ" (2 Thessalonians 3:5). Think through

some of the ways Jesus showed patience to His disciples
. . . and to others.

4. Think through the subject of protection as it is reflected in this chapter. When is it good to engage in protection, and when might it be damaging to the person involved?
5. What impresses you in the Charles Simeon quote?

Chapter 12
Keep Building

1. What were the important issues highlighted in Jesus' intercessory prayer? (John 17:15–26). What can we learn from this concerning our prayers for one another?
2. Can you recall measurable differences prayer has made in your life?
3. Consider having two people (using their imaginations) role-play the John 21 story. As a group, comment on what it has meant to you to see forgiveness pass between two people like Jesus and Simon Peter.
4. As you think back across your own experiences, what is the greatest example of giving or receiving forgiveness that you remember?
5. What are some of the attitudes and habits which are fostered in our culture that make forgiveness and restoration difficult today?

Chapter 13
Celebrating Intimacy

1. How is sexual intimacy a celebration of the past, present, and future of a marriage?
2. Discuss the principles and implications of Paul's teaching in 1 Thessalonians 4:3–8. How does this clash with contemporary values in secular society?

239

3. Which of the Hebrew verbs used for sexual activity (*see* comments on these words in the chapter) describe today's cultural perspective?
4. In what ways do husbands and wives seem to differ in their approach to sexuality in marriage?
5. Describe the contrast between the climb to the top and the tramway ride to the top of the mountain. Of what significance has this metaphor been to you?

Chapter 14
The Days We Remember, and the Ones We'd Like to Forget

1. Review the "parallels" mentioned in this chapter. What is the significance of each?
2. Why are the parallels between a person's journey of faith and a person's journey with his or her spouse so significant?
3. As an aid in relating to others, what has been the most helpful portion of this book for you?